T0170430

Abraham among the Yankees

Abraham Lincoln, 1846. LIBRARY OF CONGRESS.

ABRAHAM AMONG THE YANKEES

Lincoln's 1848 Visit to Massachusetts

William F. Hanna

Foreword by Frank J. Williams

Southern Illinois University Press
Carbondale

Southern Illinois University Press
www.siupress.com

First published 1983 by the Old Colony Historical Society, Taunton,
Massachusetts. Southern Illinois University Press edition 2020.
Printed in the United States of America

23 22 21 20   4 3 2 1

Cover illustration: Abraham Lincoln, 1846 (cropped). LIBRARY OF
CONGRESS.

Library of Congress Cataloging-in-Publication Data
Names: Hanna, William F., author. | Williams, Frank J., writer of
    foreword.
Title: Abraham among the Yankees : Lincoln's 1848 visit to
    Massachusetts / William F. Hanna ; foreword by Frank J. Williams.
Description: Southern Illinois University Press edition. | Carbondale
    : Southern Illinois University Press, 2020. | "First published 1983
    by the Old Colony Historical Society, Taunton, Massachusetts."
    | Includes bibliographical references and index. | Summary:
    "This book details Lincoln's campaigning for Zachary Taylor
    in Massachusetts in September 1848. Using newspaper
    coverage as well as all available eyewitness accounts, this book
    recounts the complete story of Lincoln's only extended visit to
    Massachusetts"— Provided by publisher.
Identifiers: LCCN 2019036257 (print) | LCCN 2019036258 (ebook) |
    ISBN 9780809337798 (paperback) | ISBN 9780809337804 (ebook)
Subjects: LCSH: Lincoln, Abraham, 1809–1865—Travel—
    Massachusetts.
Classification: LCC E457.4 .H36 2020 (print) | LCC E457.4 (ebook) |
    DDC 973.7092—dc23
LC record available at https://lccn.loc.gov/2019036257
LC ebook record available at https://lccn.loc.gov/2019036258

Printed on recycled paper ♻

In memory of my father

. . . a capital specimen of a "Sucker" Whig, six feet at least in his stockings.
>   —Boston *Atlas*, September 22, 1848

Yes, I had been chosen to Congress then from the wild West, and with hayseed in my hair I went to Massachusetts, the most cultured State in the Union, to take a few lessons in deportment.
>   —President Abraham Lincoln, 1861

Contents

Illustrations

Foreword

William F. Hanna, a loyal and hardworking member of the Lincoln Group of Boston, has written an interesting and fast paced account of Abraham Lincoln's first visit to Massachusetts in 1848. It was an important visit — important for Lincoln's growth, exposure and work in the political vineyards and important for the Whig party. General Zachary Taylor's Whig candidacy for the Presidency that year deeply divided many Whigs — with Whig defections to the newly formed Free Soil party. Despite his personal misgivings, Lincoln was true to party loyalty and supported the Taylor candidacy — even over that of his hero, Henry Clay.

Lincoln was one of several stump speakers sent North to bolster Taylor's chances for victory. This is a most cogent account of Lincoln's mission to Massachusetts. From Lowell to Taunton, Lincoln spoke the party line and was well received by the press and those who heard him.

Mr. Hanna has searched newspapers and other primary sources for accounts of Lincoln's visits to nine Bay State communities where he made twelve speeches over a period of eleven days. Everywhere he went, Lincoln fought against the defections of Whigs to the opposition — arguing that the Free Soil party could not win, but could take away enough votes from the Whigs to cause a loss of the election.

This small, well written volume is amply illustrated and annotated. It is a refreshing addition to Lincolniana in general and to the study of Lincoln as a politician in particular.

Frank J. Williams
President
Lincoln Group of Boston

Hope Valley, Rhode Island
September 22, 1983

Introduction

In the fall of 1848 Abraham Lincoln, a little-known congressman from Illinois, spent eleven days touring eastern Massachusetts. The Whig Party, of which Lincoln was a loyal member, had nominated General Zachary Taylor for the presidency, a move that was deeply unpopular in New England. Lincoln came to the Bay State to speak on behalf of his party's nominee.

Midway through his single term in Congress, the Illinoisan had thus far done little to distinguish himself. Like most Whigs, he was opposed to the war with Mexico, so it was left to him and a host of other campaigners to explain how an apolitical neophyte such as Taylor could possibly be fit for the presidency. To Massachusetts liberals in a badly divided Whig Party, the fact that Taylor's fame had come solely because of his military exploits was proof positive that the party had abandoned all principle in favor of craven opportunism. Ever the pragmatist, Lincoln and other apologists traveled the state arguing that because of his national reputation, Taylor would win the White House, and in the end his administration would be better for the country than that of the Democratic Party's nominee, Lewis Cass, of Michigan.

In 1848 no one had any notion that the future would look on Abraham Lincoln as one of America's great figures. Thus our information about his visit, especially first-hand accounts, is not as complete as we would wish. On one hand, we are regrettably forced to rely heavily on contemporary newspaper stories, and these were notoriously biased. In another sense, however, this is entirely appropriate, because the Lincoln who came to Massachusetts in 1848 was an unsparing partisan warrior. On the stump, he pulled no punches, and those looking for an early glimpse of the author of the Gettysburg Address or the Second Inaugural will not find him in these pages. The 1848 Lincoln used humor, sarcasm, and ridicule to great advantage, but those few witnesses who in later years recalled his visit remembered him not so much for *what* he said but rather for the *way* in which he said it. Lincoln's audiences may have roared with delight as he roasted both Cass and the Free Soil Party's nominee, former president Martin Van Buren, but it was strictly style over substance.

Zachary Taylor carried Massachusetts and the nation, much to the delight of party regulars. Among them was Lincoln, who, having completed his agreed-upon single congressional term, had returned to Illinois hoping that his loyal service on Taylor's behalf would yield an appointment as commissioner of public lands. In this he was to be twice disappointed when he learned that not only had he been passed over but also the job had gone to Justin Butterfield, an Illinois rival who had done practically nothing to secure Taylor's election. After declining a couple of other patronage positions, Lincoln retired to Springfield and resumed the practice of law.

Although little attention has heretofore been given to Lincoln's Bay State visit, a couple of misconceptions must be corrected. After her husband's death, Mary Lincoln recalled that she had accompanied him on the trip to Massachusetts. In several decades of research, this author has found no contemporary evidence to support that claim. By all accounts, as he traveled the state, Lincoln was a man alone. Neither those who dealt with him directly nor the correspondents who covered his appearances for the press ever mentioned the presence of a companion. Likewise, Doris Kearns Goodwin, in her excellent book *Team of Rivals*, states that after the Tremont Temple campaign rally, Lincoln and William Seward shared a hotel room where they discussed politics long into the night. In all of the years of research into the subject of Lincoln's 1848 visit, the author of this work has seen no contemporary evidence of that assertion.

Finally, I became interested in the subject of Lincoln in Massachusetts more than forty years ago, and when this book was originally published in 1983, I was careful to include the names of those who had assisted my research. Since then, and in the preparation of this edition, I have encountered many others—from a new generation of scholars and archivists—whose help has been essential to the project. I am pleased to place their names alongside their earlier counterparts as I again extend my deepest thanks.

My old friends the Honorable Frank J. Williams and Dr. Thomas R. Turner have been interested in my work from the beginning, and I owe them a continuing debt of gratitude. Both are accomplished Lincoln scholars and their help with the present volume is much appreciated. Likewise, another fine Lincoln scholar, Dr. James Tackach, president of the Lincoln Group of Boston, has been helpful throughout the entire process, and for his support I am deeply appreciative. I will always owe a debt of gratitude to my friend and mentor the late Dr. Jordan D. Fiore, who introduced me to this subject as a young graduate student.

At Southern Illinois University Press, it has been a pleasure to work with executive editor Sylvia Frank Rodrigue and acquisitions assistant Jennifer Egan. Also, at the Library of Congress, Jonathan Eaker was most helpful in offering illustrations from that extensive collection. Closer to home, in Massachusetts, Aaron Schmidt, of the Boston Public Library, was prompt and helpful in offering advice on that institution's holdings. Katie MacDonald, Lisa Compton, and Carolyn Owen-Leary of the Old Colony History Museum in Taunton were generous with their time and expertise. Joyce Tracy and Frederick E. Bauer Jr., at the American Antiquarian Society in Worcester, accommodated every request, while nearby, at the Worcester Historical Museum, Wendy Essery and Jessica Goss helped locate photographs from their collection. At Old Sturbridge Village, Caitlin Emery Avenia and Caroline Nash were prompt and helpful in dealing with my requests. At the University of Massachusetts at Lowell, Janine Whitcomb and her predecessor, Martha Mayo, were most obliging, as were Robert McLeod of the Lowell Historical Society, and local historian Brad Parker. Robert Collins, of the Chelsea Public Library, was helpful and so was Ann Porter, of the Cambridge Public Library. At the New Bedford Free Public Library, Janice Hodson quickly answered my every request, and at the New Bedford Whaling Museum, it was a pleasure to work with Mark Procknik and Ashleigh Almeida. Last but never least, I owe sincere thanks to Rebecca Carpenter and Robert Hanson, of the Dedham Historical Society, for their gracious assistance.

Thirty-six years ago, on completing the manuscript for *Abraham among the Yankees*, I acknowledged my wife Carol for her cheerful forbearance as we traveled throughout Massachusetts in search of Lincoln. These many years later, I thank her again, for that journey and for all those that have come since.

William F. Hanna

Taunton, Massachusetts
April 15, 2019

Abraham among the Yankees

Itinerary

September 12–13	Worcester
September 14	New Bedford
September 15	Boston
September 16–18	Lowell
September 18	Dorchester
September 19	Chelsea
September 20	Dedham
	Cambridge
September 21	Taunton
September 22	Boston

CHAPTER I
PRELUDE: THE WHIGS IN TURMOIL

Autumn was gaining on New England as the Norwich train made its way north toward Worcester, Massachusetts. As the early morning sun warmed the passing countryside, Congressman Abraham Lincoln cast his eyes for the first time upon the gentle hills of Worcester County. It was September 12, 1848 and Lincoln, as he usually did, was traveling alone. His journey, begun in Washington three days earlier, would eventually take him home to Springfield, Illinois, but not before he attended to urgent business in the Bay State.

The state through which Lincoln was riding was in a period of dynamic growth, and he would see its evidence everywhere he went. Cities and towns were burgeoning, pushing the population of the Commonwealth toward the 1,000,000 mark.[1] Thirty-three thousand people lived and worked in Lowell, for example, and this was a city which had not even existed in 1825.[2] Likewise, during the same period the population of Chelsea had increased by 272%; New Bedford's had risen by 206%; Cambridge had witnessed an increase of 155%; and Worcester, Lincoln's destination on this morning, had seen its population rise by 153%.[3]

The towns through which Lincoln passed were almost always in need of labor. A skilled hand could usually find work in the construction of buildings or ships, or in the production of heavy machinery. The unskilled found jobs on the docks of Boston, New Bedford or Nantucket. At worst, if a man was willing to break his back for low pay, he could dig ditches for the state's ever-expanding network of highways and railroads.

Yet more than anything else, Lincoln was visiting a place which was centered around the cotton textile industry. Serious, profitable industrialization had come during the first two decades of the nineteenth century, especially after Francis Cabot Lowell and his Boston Associates were able to duplicate the British textile system efficiently and economically. When their first mill at Waltham proved successful, this and other groups dotted Massachusetts with factories. Wherever fast-flowing streams were available, cotton textile mills appeared. In the northern part of the state Lowell, Lawrence and Haverhill built mills. In the southeast, Taunton and Fall River were heavily industrialized, while even in western Massachusetts a factory had been built at Chicopee. Between 1810 and 1837 the state had witnessed a five-fold increase in the number of cotton textile mills.[4]

Perhaps Lincoln knew this; he was an avid newspaper reader and a man of boundless curiosity. But as he came north he realized that it was politics which was keeping him on the road. If events unfolded as he hoped they would, a few more days would not matter much. Besides, as a loyal member of the Whig party he realized that in this Presidential election year the political situation in Massachusetts was critical and demanded his attention.

Massachusetts, like Lincoln, had been married to the Whig party for a long time. Organized in 1834, the party was made up of former National Republicans, Anti-Masons and some Democrats. The common thread which bound them all together was stout opposition to the policies of President Andrew Jackson.[5]

The Whigs' belief in a strong protective tariff brought them many New England friends who shared their pro-business outlook. Native American workers saw the tariff as good job insurance against foreign competition, and farmers, especially those whose sheep provided wool for local factories, felt the same way. Also, the party found allies among those whose prosperity depended upon strong urban markets.[6]

Lincoln was certainly aware of the Whig party's ascendancy in Massachusetts. They were so successful in the period from 1834 to 1848 that with the exception of only two years the Whigs annually elected their candidate for governor. In every year but one they controlled both houses of the state legislature. Every United States Senator, and twenty-seven out of the thirty-one persons serving in the Massachusetts delegation to the House of Representatives were Whigs.[7]

It was also true that from the first the party was controlled by the cotton textile manufacturers, and they were conservative men. With the slavery issue taking on increased importance, they worked hard to maintain sectional harmony. This desire came not only from their sincere national spirit; it was also a matter of practical business necessity. Their mills could not run without Southern cotton, nor could their brother merchants afford to sacrifice the lucrative coastal trade.[8]

Throughout the first decade of its life the leadership of the Massachusetts Whig party fell to distinguished men of national reputation. In the U. S. Senate they were represented by Daniel Webster, the "god-like Daniel," a man with a booming voice and a taste for rich living. Also among their number were Rufus Choate, one of the keenest and most successful legalists of the day; Nathan Appleton and his friends William and Abbott Lawrence, textile magnates; Edward Everett, Harvard professor and former Whig Governor of Massachusetts; and Robert C. Winthrop, a descendant of Puritans as well as Lincoln's congressional colleague and Speaker of the national House of Representatives.

Yet the Massachusetts Whig party was breaking apart in the fall of 1848, and this was what had put Lincoln on the train for New England. It seems that a younger, more idealistic element had bolted the party and this threatened to wreck the Whig chances in November. Events had deeply troubled party leaders in Washington, and particularly worrisome was the fact that among these dissidents were some of the most brilliant men in the nation. What they lacked in influence they made up in talent. Their ranks included Charles Francis Adams, son and grandson of Presidents and himself a member of the Great and General Court; John A. Andrew and Anson Burlingame, two very able young lawyers, each of whom would come to prominence within the next decade; Richard Henry Dana, already celebrated for his book *Two Years Before the Mast;* John Gorham Palfrey, former publisher of the *North American Review;* and Charles Sumner and Henry Wilson, both destined for national prominence in the years immediately ahead.[9]

Also to this list could be added some of the truly distinguished minds in America, men like William Cullen Bryant, John Greenleaf Whittier, Henry Wadsworth Longfellow and James Russell Lowell. Their leading spokesman in Congress, former President John Quincy Adams, had just been lost. Indeed Congressman Lincoln had been present on the floor of the House the preceding February to witness the fatal stroke which had silenced the old gladiator for good.

In those days it seemed that all roads led to the slavery problem, and this was the issue that was slowly killing the Whig party. Hard feelings extended back to 1836 and the beginning of the Texas question. Most Massachusetts Whigs, liberals and conservatives, had opposed the acquisition of Texas. The party regulars feared that it would mean a shift in power from North to South. They believed that even if Northern political and economic dominance was impossible, at least some sort of sectional balance should be maintained. Texas, they feared, would upset that balance and send the fruits of political power rolling southward.

They also opposed annexation on constitutional grounds. They believed that while the Constitution protected slavery in those states where it already existed, it also clearly prohibited its extension beyond its present limits.[10] In this they were adamant, and their views coincided exactly with those of Abraham Lincoln.

To the young liberals, however, the annexation of Texas meant something else entirely. They saw it as a boldface attempt to perpetuate slavery and extend its territory. They considered slavery a national disgrace, even in those places where it already existed.

Although all Massachusetts Whigs wanted the same thing — Texas to remain separated from the United States — they emphasized different aspects of the problem. To the older, more conservative party members it was an economic and constitutional battle. To the young idealists it was a moral war, a holy war, and they waged it with increasing vehemence.

After several years of delay President John Tyler, on March 1, 1845, signed the bill admitting Texas to the Union. Although he would leave office in just three days, Tyler was to be followed by James Polk, an ardent expansionist, so for all practical purposes the Texas question was decided.[11]

To the conservative Whigs such as Webster, Choate and Winthrop, continued agitation over Texas would be worse than fruitless. It would only further divide the party and alienate Southern Congressmen at a time when Polk was trying to lower the tariff, something which would hurt New England deeply. They also knew that further public protest would cut them off from patronage, the staff of a politician's life.[12] Looking ahead to 1848 they realized that some semblance of national party unity had to exist if their man was to stand a chance. Significant also was their belief that further opposition would push them into closer contact with the abolitionists, at least in the eyes of Southerners, whose "King Cotton" they needed to keep their factories running.

The liberals were unmoved and refused to relent. Because theirs was a moral and not a political battle, they had no use for subtlety and no need for farsightedness. Calling themselves the "Conscience Whigs," they moved closer to the abolitionist camp and their criticism of the conservative "Cotton Whigs" became increasingly more strident. They charged the old-timers with selling out to the Southern slaveholders for the sake of economic gain.[13]

Although the Cotton Whigs considered Texas a dead issue, the Mexicans did not, and war followed in May, 1846. Just as with slavery, most Massachusetts Whigs detested the thought of a war with Mexico. The conservatives thought it was a tragic mistake, but believed that once the U. S. became committed it was the duty of Congress and the nation to support the troops in the field. Daniel Webster spoke for them when he said, "We may think a war unnecessary or unjust; but if a majority think it to be otherwise, we must submit, because we have agreed that a majority shall govern."[14]

The Conscience men, on the other hand, saw the war as a clear case of aggression for the sake of gaining more territory. They violently attacked the war as a guise to extend slavery, and they opposed every phase of its prosecution.

But as Congressman Lincoln made ready to meet the people of Worcester, he knew that it was not the Texas dispute or even the Mexican War which had finally broken the Whig party. The last straw had come just three months earlier, in a crowded, sweaty Philadelphia convention hall. There the Whigs had nominated a political neophyte, a Louisiana slaveholding general, as their candidate for the presidency. More than 135 years later it seems strange to note that Abraham Lincoln came to Massachusetts to campaign for his election.

CHAPTER II
OLD ROUGH AND READY

The story goes that when an admirer first mentioned to Zachary Taylor that he might make a good President, the old general snapped: "Stop your nonsense and drink your whiskey!"[1] This was good advice, but as the weeks went by even Taylor could not adhere to it. On the night of June 6, 1848, in Philadelphia's Chinese Museum, the Mexican War hero was handed the Whig party's nomination for the presidency. Millard Fillmore, an old party regular, took the second spot on the ticket.

The Whigs could hardly have found a more unlikely candidate. At age sixty-four Taylor had spent his entire life in the military. As Albert J. Beveridge has pointed out, he could neither speak not write correctly; he knew nothing about public business or foreign affairs; and nobody knew where he stood on important issues because he had no idea himself.[2] Indeed "Old Rough and Ready" had been so far removed from politics as to admit that he had never in his life voted in a presidential election.[3]

There was more. Besides being a principal figure in a war which most Whigs had detested, Taylor was a Southerner whose Louisiana plantation held over 100 slaves, and this made him one of a very few large slaveowners.[4]

Massachusetts Whigs, especially the Conscience men, were outraged. Within seconds after the final vote was tallied Charles Allen, a liberal from Worcester, was on his feet screaming: "We declare the Whig party of the Union this day dissolved!" In an effort to shout him down, many delegates, apparently led by Southerners, began to chant the name of a more reliable Bay Stater, "Cho-ate, Choate, CHO-ATE!"

Allen was quickly joined by Henry Wilson and as a chorus of jeers, hisses and groans filled the hall, the "Natick Cobbler" promised, "I go home and so help me God, I will do all that I can to defeat that nomination."[5] Making a final, bitter allusion to Cotton Whig Abbott Lawrence's futile wish to be Taylor's Vice-President, Allen shouted, "Massachusetts will spurn the bribe."[6] With that a decade of frustration burst forth and the

Conscience men quit the hall and the Whig party, never to return.

Watching all this from somewhere inside the Chinese Museum was Abraham Lincoln, and he knew as well as anybody why the Whigs had sacrificed their principles to nominate Taylor. It was, as Daniel Webster called it, the "Doctrine of Availability," the certain knowledge that the famous war hero would be elected.[7]

This was cynical and this was partisan, but it was quite all right with Abraham Lincoln. Ten years later, in one of his debates with Stephen A. Douglas, Lincoln referred to Henry Clay as, "my beau ideal of a statesman, the man for whom I fought all my humble life."[8] When he said this he was forgetting the 1848 campaign, because in that year he willingly tossed Clay aside when it appeared that there might be a stronger candidate on the horizon. In a letter to an Illinois friend, he had written, "Mr. Clay's chance for an election, is just no chance at all . . . In my judgment we can elect nobody but Gen. Taylor . . . ."[9]

In fact, Lincoln's interest in the Louisianan's candidacy went as far back as December, 1846. At that time he became one of the charter members of the "Young Indians," a Congressional club dedicated to winning the nomination for Taylor. Of the seven original members of this group, all but two — Lincoln and Truman Smith of Connecticut — were Southerners and friends of slavery. Likewise, most of those who later joined were from the South. A touch of irony was added to the story by the fact that one of Lincoln's closest friends in the "Young Indians" was Alexander Stephens of Georgia, later the Vice-President of the Confederacy.[10]

Lincoln, of course, was pleased with Taylor's success, and this perhaps caused him to be a bit more optimistic than he should have been. Shortly after the nomination he wrote:

> By many, and often, it had been said that they
> would not abide by the nomination of Taylor; but
> since the deed has been done, they are fast falling in,

8

Zachary Taylor. LIBRARY OF CONGRESS.

and in my opinion we shall have a most overwhelming, glorious, triumph. One unmistakable sign is, that all the odds and ends are with us — Barnburners, Native Americans, Tyler men, disappointed office seeking locofocos, and the Lord knows what.[11]

Lincoln was certainly overstating the situation in New England, and especially Massachusetts. The liberals' opposition to Taylor was broadcast throughout the state in Whig meetings, like the one in Natick which issued a typical statement at its conclusion. "We are not," it claimed, "so far degraded as to give the lie to all our past professions; to acknowledge ourselves knaves, hypocrites, slaves and fools for the sake of a Whig victory; and we do therefore repudiate the nomination of Zachary Taylor, and will do our utmost to defeat his election."[12]

On June 28 the Conscience men held a meeting in Worcester to formally announce their rejection of Taylor's candidacy. Plans were made for the national anti-slavery convention which was held in Buffalo in early August. It was there that the liberal Whigs were joined by Democrats unhappy with Lewis Cass, their party's nominee. Also attending were Barnburners, anti-slavery radicals from New York, Liberty party men from all over the North, and hundreds of others who generally opposed the extension of slavery. These "odds and ends," as Lincoln called them, formed the Free Soil party and nominated Martin Van Buren, the old "Wily Fox of Kinderhook," for the presidency. Charles Francis Adams became his running mate. This new party had real strength, despite Lincoln's rosy assessment, and in New England thousands became Free Soilers.[13]

The conservative Whig party leaders in Massachusetts were none too happy with Taylor's nomination either. On Friday, July 9, the Boston *Daily Advertiser,* a Whig paper, said that it would be of little use to disguise the fact that Taylor's selection was "far from gratifying to the great majority of Whigs of Massachusetts." While expressing personal respect for the old general, the editor nevertheless thought that "the

Martin Van Buren. LIBRARY OF CONGRESS.

people of Massachusetts have not regarded, and cannot now regard him as possessed of qualifications for the most satisfactory discharge of the duties of the office . . . ."[14]

This mirrored exactly the sentiments of most of the state's party regulars, but this was an era of fierce party loyalty, and they were seasoned politicians, accustomed to making the best out of unpleasant situations. Their position was clearly stated by Daniel Webster. Disappointed at first at having been passed over by the Philadelphia convention, he had originally seen the nomination as "not fit to be made."[15] Later, after regaining his political senses, Webster sounded the keynote for the conservatives. "The safest way is to overlook the nomination as not being the main thing," he said, "and to continue to maintain the Whig cause."[16]

This theme, stressing party unity above personal feelings, was adopted by William Schouler, the influential editor of the Boston *Atlas*. This paper promised to support the nominee, even though its editor admitted that, "we have had other preferences." Unity came first, wrote Schouler, therefore, "It matters not that he was not our choice, nor the choice of Massachusetts."[17] For the most part Schouler's colleagues around the state reluctantly followed his lead.

So the Bay State Whigs, after swallowing their scruples, prepared for a tough election campaign with a candidate they ordinarily would have held in contempt. Like Lincoln, they thought that party unity was more important than any other issue, even slavery, because it was the only way of keeping the Democrats out of the White House. They saw a Whig victory, even by a man like Zachary Taylor, as the only way of preserving a healthy future for the nation, and even perhaps of saving the Union itself.[18]

In order to win this fight the Massachusetts Whigs would need all of the outside help they could get. This began a procession of stump speakers, some famous, some hardly known, moving across the state. One of the more obscure was the tall gentleman from Illinois just arrived in Worcester and looking for a good hotel.

CHAPTER III
WORCESTER

As the autumn sun began its slide toward dusk, lamplighters moved along the streets firing the whale oil pots which cast their soft light down on the crowds thronging the sidewalks. A carnival atmosphere prevailed in Worcester on September 12, 1848, the eve of the Whig state convention. The city's population of eleven and a half thousand would swell this night by thousands more, every tavern and hotel filled with visitors.[1] Delegates, candidates, brass bands and hangers-on contested each other and the natives for the limited sidewalk space. Each arriving train brought new contenders, and all of this only added to the merriment.

Alone among the crowd was Abraham Lincoln. The thirty-nine year old freshman Congressman was for the most part unknown to New Englanders. True, he had met a few Whig leaders from the Northeast at the Philadelphia convention, but most of his contact with them had come through letters. In August he had corresponded twice with William Schouler, editor of the Boston *Atlas*. The first time he had asked "Friend Schooler [sic]" for his "undisguised opinion" regarding Taylor's chances in New England, and particularly Massachusetts. Later he thanked him and offered a brief analysis of Illinois politics.[2]

Lincoln had likewise been in touch with Junius Hall, a Boston attorney who apparently invited him to speak in the Bay State. He told Hall that he expected to travel to Boston but was unsure about Worcester because he was "somewhat impatient to go home now."[3] However after Congress adjourned on August 14, Lincoln stayed in Washington to finish up some campaign work and then, probably at the urging of the Whig Central Committee, set a course for Worcester.

It is interesting that the Whigs chose this central Massachusetts city for their state convention, for nowhere in the Commonwealth was the Free Soil party as strong as it was here.[4] Settled in 1722 and incorporated as a city just six months before Lincoln's visit, Worcester was growing rapidly. Although some 2,000 people worked in its factories,[5] it nevertheless maintained a rural flavor upon which the Free Soil movement thrived. Charles Allen, the Worcesterite who had so recently declared the Whig party dead in Philadelphia, had returned home to a rousing welcome. A huge meeting was held on the Common and after several fiery speeches it was decided that Massachusetts should forever "go for free soil and free men, for free lips, for free land, and a free world."[6]

Such an ambitious proposal left little room for the likes of Zachary Taylor, and his candidacy promised to fall flat in Worcester County. The editor of the *National Aegis,* the local Whig newspaper, expressed regret that Taylor had been chosen over Webster, but still quietly promised to support the ticket.[7] The *Massachusetts Spy,* a respected journal since the days of the Revolution, said that although greatly disappointed by the nomination, it would not allow itself to be driven from its traditional support of the Whig cause.[8] This resolution was short-lived, however, for within two months the *Spy* would be found firmly entrenched among the Free Soilers.

The *Palladium,* Worcester's Democratic newspaper, agreed with Charles Allen's assertion that the Whig party was finished, and the editor saw it as suicide. Taylor's nomination, he wrote, "puts at defiance all calculations upon the probabilities of human conduct. Who could have believed it possible? But little have they ever known of him. But little do they know of him even now." It seemed, said the editor, that the party had grown tired, "and willing [that] it should be dissolved . . . ."[9]

As the pre-convention crowds swarmed through Worcester, Alexander Bullock was a man with a problem. In his role as chairman of the local Whig committee, he had called for a public rally to be held at City Hall that evening. Knowing that many prominent Whigs would be in town, he had invited several to make speeches. By sundown he knew that none had accepted. Just then someone told him that an Illinois

Lewis Cass. LIBRARY OF CONGRESS.

Congressman named Lincoln was in town, and within minutes the chairman was busy tracking down the visitor.[10]

Bullock found Lincoln at the Worcester House, on the corner of Main and Elm Streets. In 1848 this building was one of the best hotels in town, but in the old days it had been the mansion of former Massachusetts Governor Levi Lincoln. In those times it had hosted such notables as Lafayette, John Quincy Adams, Daniel Webster and Henry Clay.[11]

The Whig chairman explained the situation to Lincoln and asked him to speak that evening. Lincoln, according to Bullock, "readily assented," and the problem was solved.[12]

No word-for-word account of Lincoln's Massachusetts speeches exists, but we nevertheless have a good idea of what he said. In his letter to Junius Hall, Lincoln wrote that he had "the elements of one speech in mind, which I should like to deliver to a community politically affected as I understand yours to be . . . ."[13] He was referring to a speech which he had delivered on the floor of the House the preceding July. This was an old-fashioned, hard-hitting stump speech, and newspaper accounts show that he adhered to it throughout the campaign. He was eager to try it out on a Yankee audience.

At promptly 7 p.m. Lincoln strode into City Hall wearing a long linen duster. The reporter for the Boston *Daily Advertiser* saw a man with "a very tall and thin figure, with an intellectual face, showing a searching mind, and a cool judgement."[14] As he faced his audience, one reporter estimated that at least 1,000 people were jammed inside the room to hear him.[15]

Lincoln was introduced by Ensign H. Kellogg, of Pittsfield, who noted that he was a member of the "Central Executive Committee at Washington." He was also presented as a representative of "free soil," and he said nothing to dispute this. He began by expressing a sense of modesty at being invited to speak "this side of the mountains," where everybody was so instructed and wise.[16]

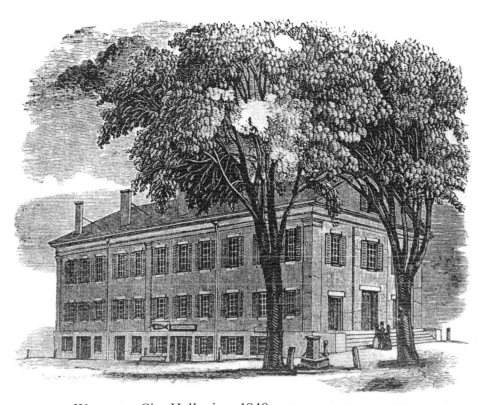

Worcester City Hall, circa 1848. FROM THE COLLECTION OF THE
WORCESTER HISTORICAL MUSEUM, WORCESTER, MASSACHUSETTS.

Lincoln's message in Worcester, and throughout Massachusetts, was twofold. First, he was anxious to show that Taylor, despite his background, was indeed a man of genuine Whig principles. He quoted from a letter which the nominee had written to J. R. Allison, expressing some of the most general views on government. Taylor said that a President's personal preferences should always remain secondary. The will of the people, as expressed through their elected representatives, should take precedence over anything the President might think. The reporter for the *Springfield Republican* remembered Lincoln saying that this "was the greatest and best principle that could be advanced or maintained by any party." In a remarkable display of expediency, Lincoln said that Taylor's advocacy of this principle put him in advance of even Henry Clay. "Gen. Taylor's ground and the Whig ground," said Lincoln, "is that the people ought to do as they please in regard to all questions of domestic policy . . . ." Clay "was and always is ready to give his opinions and preferences, and thus would present motives for others to prostitute themselves to gain favor with him, if in power."[17] How strange this sounds from a man who would go down in history as one of the strongest American Presidents.

The Whigs had not bothered to adopt a platform at the Philadelphia convention, and in justifying this Lincoln turned an about-face on traditional Whig policy. Taylor, he said, maintained a sound, republican principle which, it was shown, was "far more preferable and far more useful to the great majority of the country than the variegated and impractical 'platforms' that it had become the fashion . . . to adopt."[18] This was pure posturing, for the Whigs had always prided themselves on their well defined campaign platforms.

Second, Lincoln was in Massachusetts as much to speak *against* Van Buren as he was to speak *for* Taylor. The message which he repeated time and again was that Van Buren could not win the presidency; all he could do was take enough votes away from Taylor to give Cass the election, and a Democrat in the White House would surely mean the extension of slavery. It was the Democratic party, he claimed, which had annexed all of the new territory, and how foolish it was for the Free Soilers to aid them further. Their claim that they would "do their duty and leave the consequences to God," was, said Lincoln, merely a way to justify a course of action which they could not maintain by fair argument.[19]

As for slavery, Lincoln told the audience that the people of Illinois felt the same as the people of New England, "except perhaps that they did not keep so constantly thinking about it." Most Whigs believed that slavery was wrong, he said, but it was also a fact that nothing could be done about it where it already existed. The fight should be centered on keeping it within its present boundaries, and only a Whig victory could ensure that.

Finally, Lincoln tried to turn the tables on the Van Burenites by claiming that theirs was the party without principles. It was true, he said, that they were anti-slavery, but if they held any other ideas they were like the pair of pantaloons offered by a Yankee peddler, "large enough for any man, small enough for any boy."[20]

Newspaper coverage of the speech was decidedly partisan. Samuel Bowles' *Springfield Republican* gave a glowing account of the meeting. Noting that the hall was "well filled in all parts and crowded in some," the writer said that he had never seen "a more gratifying, interesting, and encouraging Whig gathering" in Massachusetts. The reporter noted that Lincoln was "frequently interrupted by loud cheering, and an incidental allusion to WEBSTER brought out immense applause."[21]

The writer for the *National Aegis,* whatever he thought of Taylor, was also genuinely enthusiastic about Lincoln's address when he said that, "For sound conclusive reasoning, and ready wit, it is unsurpassed in the campaign." He noted that the speaker and the speech were cheered repeatedly, in spite of an appearance by the "Free Lips Party," apparent hecklers.[22]

19

The Boston Whig papers were also impressed with Lincoln's talk. William Schouler, in the pages of his Boston *Atlas,* said that the meeting was large and enthusiastic and that Lincoln spoke for upwards of two hours. "Gentlemen inform me that it was one of the best speeches ever heard in Worcester," wrote Schouler, "and that several Whigs, who had gone off on the 'Free Soil' sizzle, have come back again to the Whig ranks." The *Daily Advertiser* called it a "truly masterly and convincing speech," while the *Courier* noted that it had been a "great meeting" at which the "best spirit prevailed." Finally, the Boston *Herald* said that lack of space prevented it from giving a full account of the rally, but that it represented "A TREMENDOUS VOICE FOR TAYLOR AND FILLMORE."[23]

Even the Worcester *Palladium,* a Democratic paper, had to give grudging credit to the speech. The editor admitted that "Whiggery in the Old Bay State is a hard thing to kill," and he cited the reaction to Lincoln's address as proof.[24]

Henry J. Gardner, who would become the Know Nothing Governor of Massachusetts in 1855, was in City Hall that night and heard Lincoln. He remembered that:

> No one had ever heard him on the stump, and in fact knew anything about him. When he was announced, his tall, angular, bent form, and his manifest awkwardness and low tone of voice, promised nothing interesting. But soon he warmed to his work. His style and manner of speaking were novelties in the East. He repeated anecdotes, told stories admirable in humor and in point, interspersed with bursts of true eloquence, which constantly brought down the house. His sarcasm of Cass, Van Buren and the Democratic party was inimitable, and whenever he attempted to stop, the shouts of 'Go on! go on!' were deafening. He probably spoke over an hour, but so great was the enthusiasm time could not be measured. It was doubtless one of the best efforts of his life.[25]

For all this, there appear to have been some listeners whom Lincoln offended that evening. When Bullock invited him to speak earlier in the day, he had explained to Lincoln that there were many Free Soilers in Worcester County, and he asked him to use "much discretion" in his remarks.[26] Lincoln had agreed, but during the course of his speech he made an off-hand comment which hurt many of the anti-slavery men in the crowd. "I have heard you have abolitionists here," said Lincoln, who then noted that they were "better treated" in New England than elsewhere. Turning to a man on the platform who had lived in the Mid-West, Lincoln continued, "We have a few in Illinois, and we shot one the other day." The Free Soilers thought that the remark was "heartless," and Lincoln did not repeat it again in Massachusetts.[27] The reference apparently was to Elijah Lovejoy, an abolitionist editor murdered by a pro-slavery mob in Alton, Illinois. However that event had taken place in 1837, hardly "the other day."

Early next morning, several hours before the Whig state convention was gaveled to order, Lincoln was around and about town. Much of his time was spent on a makeshift platform which had been built in front of the railroad station. The trains from Boston were expected to arrive at about 10 o'clock and Lincoln, in the company of the Worcester Rough and Ready Club, was present to greet the delegates and escort them to City Hall.

It was a beautiful day, and the flags and bunting hanging everywhere added to the festive spirit. The first Boston train arrived early and Lincoln, with its 500 passengers and at least one brass band, paraded through the streets around the station. When they returned to the depot to await the second train from Boston, several prominent Whigs were called upon to speak. With an estimated 800 people crowding around the platform, rousing speeches were made boosting the Whig cause. It seems that Lincoln was interrupted in the middle of his by the arrival of the train with its 500 delegates and friends.[28]

The *Massachusetts Spy,* under the pen of the ardent Free Soiler John Milton Earle, commented on the depot speeches,

Levi Lincoln. LIBRARY OF CONGRESS.

including the one by Lincoln, whom he mistakenly called the "recently defeated Taylor candidate in the 7th district in Illinois for reelection to Congress." These addresses, wrote Earle, were "rather witty, though truth and reason and argument were treated as out of the question, as unnecessary and not to be expected." When it was pointed out to the editor that the Illinoisian had not been a candidate for reelection to Congress, he wrote that Lincoln, foreseeing defeat, had "prudently withdrawn" from the contest.[29]

The state convention that day nominated George N. Briggs for governor and John Reed for lieutenant governor. Several well known Whigs, including Levi Lincoln, Rufus Choate and Robert C. Winthrop addressed the delegates. Yet the visitor from Illinois remained silent, "that day and in that body unknown and unheard," wrote Alexander Bullock.[30]

In the evening the visitor, along with several other prominent Whigs, was invited to dine at the home of former Governor Levi Lincoln. This beautiful two story white house with its six columns in front had been built in 1835, and it was the social center of Worcester.[31]

At the table with the two Lincolns that night were Henry Gardner, Rufus Choate, George Ashmun, George L. Hillard, Emory Washburn, Alexander H. Bullock, Charles L. Putnam and Stephen Salisbury. Along with Gardner, Washburn and Bullock were future Massachusetts governors.[32] Also, George Ashmun would become the chairman of the Republican National Convention in 1860. This was the Chicago convention which nominated Lincoln for the Presidency.

The conversation at dinner centered, of course, on politics and the campaign. As elder statesman of the group, Governor Lincoln guided the talk around the full spectrum of election year news and speculation, as well as of the ills which were plaguing the Whig party. The old man had seen it all, from the Texas question through annexation and the Mexican War. And if the subject of the war came up, the Governor could have

Levi Lincoln House, Worcester, Massachusetts, circa 1865.
COURTESY OF OLD STURBRIDGE VILLAGE, STURBRIDGE, MASSACHUSETTS.

Levi Lincoln House in Sturbridge, Massachusetts, 1982.

added a personal perspective on that, for his son George, a captain in the army, had perished at Buena Vista.[33] In this he shared a tragic bond with two other stalwart Whigs, Clay and Webster.

Henry Gardner, remembering the affair, said that Abraham Lincoln "kept very quiet." It was inevitable, however, that the question of kinship between the Bay State governor and the Illinois lawmaker should arise. Finally, after much joking, Abraham Lincoln said, "I hope we both belong, as the Scotch say, to the same clan; but I know one thing, and that is we are both good Whigs."[34]

Years later, in 1861, Gardner paid his respects to President Lincoln at the White House. After being introduced, Lincoln told Gardner, "You and I are no strangers; we dined together at Governor Lincoln's in 1848." Inviting his guest to sit awhile, the President continued:

Yes, I had been chosen to Congress then from the wild West, and with hayseed in my hair I went to Massachusetts, the most cultured State in the Union, to take a few lessons in deportment. That was a grand dinner — a superb dinner; by far the finest I ever saw in my life. And the great men who were there, too! Why, I can tell you just how they were arranged at table.

"He began at one end," said Gardner, "and mentioned the names in order, and, I verily believe, without the omission of a single one."[35]

All of that, however, was years in the future as Lincoln walked back through the darkness to his room at the Worcester House. His visit to New England was off to an auspicious start. He had not only spoken for Taylor, but he had also lined up several more speaking engagements all around eastern Massachusetts over the next few days. Perhaps he knew as he retired for the night that tomorrow would bring him to another Free Soil stronghold, New Bedford.

CHAPTER IV
NEW BEDFORD

Lincoln's train left Worcester early on the morning of September 14 and traveled in an easterly direction. Whether he went to New Bedford, in far southeastern Massachusetts, via Boston or Providence is unknown, but both theories have their supporters.[1] It is certain that he arrived in the city during the afternoon. The railroad station there, looking like an Egyptian temple, was located on Pearl Street, between Purchase Street and Acushnet Avenue.

While the Whig state convention provided Lincoln with the opportunity to make the acquaintance of many of the Bay State's most influential men, it also allowed him to renew old friendships. This was true in the case of Joseph Grinnell, Lincoln's colleague in the Thirtieth Congress, who was now facing a tough reelection fight. His opponent was the city's very popular mayor, Abraham Howland. Grinnell's friends, having heard Lincoln in Worcester and knowing that an appearance by a fellow Congressman would never hurt, asked him to speak in New Bedford on the evening of September 14. Having a flexible schedule and not wishing to miss an opportunity to stump for Taylor, Lincoln accepted.

Incorporated only the year before, New Bedford was just beginning to take its place among the leading economic areas of the state. Built on land which rises quickly from the Acushnet River, its population in 1848 had passed the 16,000 mark.[2]

Aside from the small farms which dotted the outlying areas, New Bedford was mainly supported by two industries. As a seaport it was surpassed in tonnage only by New York, Boston and New Orleans. In 1848 at least 250 whalers called New Bedford home, and that industry would continue to grow until 1857, when its harbor would shelter at least 329 whaleships. When Lincoln visited the city, approximately 7,000 men were engaged in whaling.[3]

More vital to the long-range economy of New Bedford was its young cotton textile industry. Manufacturing activities had started late here, but thanks to farsighted men like Joseph Grinnell, whose $10,000 headed the subscription list of the thriving Wamsutta Mills, the textile industry would one day fill the void left by the passing of the whalers.[4] In 1848, as Grinnell's mills turned their 10,000 spindles, the future looked bright indeed.[5]

New Bedford was a Whig city, but Taylor's candidacy was extremely unpopular. There was a great deal of anti-slavery sentiment here, much of it owing to a large Quaker element, and New Bedford Whigs agreed with the local party journal, the *Daily Mercury,* when it found Taylor "a candidate not acceptable to the people." The nominee was, said the editor, "a politician without principles or settled ideas of policy." The paper noted that he would be "reluctantly supported" by Bay Staters because he was "confessedly unsuited for civil office." Later the editor, still expressing deep regret over the "sacrifice of Henry Clay," promised to "bow to the decision of the majority" and support the ticket.[6]

The first public notice of Lincoln's appearance came in the *Daily Mercury* of September 14, a simple announcement stating that, "HON. A. LINCOLN, a member of Congress from Illinois, will address the Whigs of New Bedford at LIBERTY HALL, THIS EVENING."[7]

The meeting hall in which Lincoln spoke was a strange place to boost the candidacy of a Louisiana slaveholder. A large wooden structure on the corner of Purchase and William Streets, it had been built in 1795. In 1838 it was sold by the Unitarian Society and named Liberty Hall. It became a hotbed of abolitionism and regularly hosted speakers like William Lloyd Garrison, Wendell Phillips, Frederick Douglass and Theodore Parker. It was said that the bell in the tower was used to warn fugitive slaves of the approach of the authorities.[8] Its location in the heart of New Bedford made it a favorite of political groups wanting to stage rallies.

Lincoln was to speak at a meeting called to ratify the

Joseph Grinnell. COURTESY OF THE NEW BEDFORD WHALING MUSEUM.

actions of the city's delegates to the Worcester convention. The proceedings began promptly at 7:30 p.m. As expected, the report of the delegation was heartily endorsed and, after a speech by Congressman Grinnell, the chairman introduced Lincoln. Unfortunately, no one took detailed notes of the talk, but it appears that the speech adhered pretty closely to the one given in Worcester's City Hall. The reporter for the *Daily Mercury,* though not keen on Taylor, was very much taken with the Illinois Congressman. He wrote that Lincoln had made a "most admirable and effective speech," and had "enchained the attention of a delighted audience for nearly two hours." "His speech covered the whole ground of the national election," said the *Mercury,* "and was marked by great originality, clear, conclusive, convincing reasoning and enlivened by frequent flashes of genuine, racy western wit." The reporter noted that the audience was unusually attentive, and he credited that to the effectiveness of Lincoln's arguments. "In fact," wrote the *Mercury* man, "he took the house right between the wind and the water." At the conclusion of the speech, which the writer thought would have "a lasting impression" on the audience, Lincoln sat down amidst a round of hearty cheers.[9]

Although the newspaper reporter enjoyed himself, there is evidence that at least one person present in Liberty Hall did not. He was Samuel Rodman, a Quaker, whose diary that day recorded, " . . . in the evening went to a Whig meeting which was addressed by Mr. Lincoln of Illinois. It was pretty sound, but not a tasteful speech."[10]

That evening after the meeting Lincoln was taken to the home of Congressman Grinnell, where he stayed the night. This beautiful stone mansion, located on County Street, befitted a man of Grinnell's prominence. As the sixty year old banker, legislator, industrialist and railroad president looked back over his fruitful public life, he could not know that he would outlive his Illinois guest by fully twenty years, dying at the age of ninety-seven in 1885.[11] In any event, he sent Lincoln on his way to Boston early on the morning of Sept. 15, 1848.

Joseph Grinnell Mansion. COURTESY OF THE NEW BEDFORD WHALING MUSEUM.

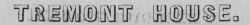

TREMONT HOUSE.

BILL OF FARE.

Table D'Hote, August 30, 1847.

Tomato Soup.

Boiled Salmon, Anchovy Sauce,
    "   Corned Beef and Cabbage,
    "   Ham, Madeira Sauce,
    "   Leg of Mutton, Caper Sauce,
    "   Calf's Head and Pluck, Brain Sauce,
    "—Chickens and Oyster Sauce.

Paté aux huitres,
Ris de veau aux petits pois,
Mayonnaise de volaille,
Cotelettes de mouton à la anglaise,
Paté de pigeons,
Anguilles à l'espagnole,
Canards aux haricots,
Rouleau de porc aux olives,
Hachis de boeuf-salé,
Maquereau grillé à la maitre d'hotel,
Aubergines frites au naturel,
Fricandeau de veau à la jardinière,
Rognons de boeuf sautés au vin de champagne,
Pigeons grillés à la sauce piquante,
Amourettes de mouton frites,
Ragout de veau aux pommes de terre,
Beignets soufflés,
Haricot de mouton,
Brocheton cuit au vin rouge,
Macaroni au jus.

Roast Beef,	Roast Ducks,
" Pork,	" Turkies,
" Lamb, Mint Sauce,	" Chickens,
" Geese,	" Grouse.

Potatoes,   Green Corn,   Squash,   Onions,
Beets,   Cucumbers,   Shelled Beans,   Turnips,
                    Tomatoes.

Bread Puddings,   Squash Pies,   Tomato Pies,   Apple Pies,
Peach Pies,   Blanc Mange,   Apple Puffs,   Berry Pies.

Apples,   Peaches,   Whortleberries,   Minorca Melons,   Almonds,
Plums,   Pecan Nuts,   Raisins,   Filberts,   Hickory Nuts,
                Watermelons.

Eastburn's Press.

Tremont House bill of fare, 1847. LIBRARY OF CONGRESS.

CHAPTER V
BOSTON: WASHINGTON HALL

The Boston which Abraham Lincoln saw for perhaps the first time on September 15 was a small city both in population (130,000) and area. In 1847 Boston did not have even one horsecar. Instead, the city and its environs were connected by a series of stagecoach lines. Likewise, workers had just begun laying water pipes, a project which had encountered some opposition from local residents. The city and its suburbs supported seventy-five newspapers, but the aggregate circulation was very small.

Physically too, the Boston of 1848 was a different city. The present day Back Bay area, including those streets which now stretch from the Public Garden, was in 1848 either swampland or completely under water. The Public Garden itself had only recently been reclaimed from the marshes.[1]

Abraham Lincoln may have been a prairie lawyer, but whenever he had the opportunity he tested New England's finest hotels. He walked from the railroad station, up Tremont Street to the elegant Tremont House, which would be his base of operations for the next few days. Opened in 1829, this was a beautiful hotel which had sheltered, among others, Henry Clay, Andrew Jackson, Commodore Isaac Hull and Charles Dickens. When Lincoln walked out the front door, just a few steps to his right was the entrance to the Old Granary Burial Ground, which held the bones of Hancock, Revere and many other Revolutionary patriots.[2]

A short, pleasant walk would have brought him to the State House, with its golden dome overlooking Beacon Hill as it sloped down to the Boston Common. This neighborhood, from Charles Street, up Beacon Street to the State Capitol, was a bastion of conservative aristocracy and would have shown Lincoln some of the most beautiful homes and gardens in Boston. Oliver Wendell Holmes once described Beacon Street as "the sunny street which holds the sifted few." It was said that there were still a few old-timers in this neighborhood who thought that America had made a serious mistake in parting from Great Britain.[3]

Lincoln's first Boston speech was delivered before the Boston Whig Club, also called the Young Men's Whig Club, an organization whose headquarters were on Bromfield Street. Two Whig newspapers, the *Atlas* and the *Courier,* both advertised the talk in the editions of that day. The *Atlas* hoped that the meeting would be "a rouser," while the *Courier* said that all friends of Taylor and Fillmore were invited to the rally.[4]

The New England weather had taken on its typical unpredictability as Lincoln arrived. On Thursday, as he spoke in New Bedford, Lincoln was treated to a wintry blast, with coal fires and heavy coats needed to keep warm. Yet the next day, according to the *Herald,* the atmosphere was as "bland and beautiful as that of a Mohammedan's Paradise."[5]

Only two Boston newspapers covered the speech, but each story adds something to the picture of Lincoln in New England. The Boston *Atlas,* edited by "Friend Schooler [sic]," gives us an overview of Lincoln's two-pronged campaign pitch. First, regarding Taylor's qualifications for the Presidency, the paper said that Lincoln, with much feeling,

> defended General Taylor from the charge that he had no principles, by showing conclusively that his avowed and well known principles were, that the people's will should be obeyed, and not frustrated by Executive usurpation and the interposition of the veto power.

Then, just as importantly, Lincoln went after the Free Soilers:

> He pointed out the absurdity of men who professed Whig principles supporting Van Buren, with all his Locofocoism, while the Whigs were as much opposed to the extension of slavery as were the Van Buren party.

Whig Party campaign banner, 1848. LIBRARY OF CONGRESS.

The *Atlas* continued to praise the speech, saying that it contained "sound reasoning, cogent argument and keen satire, which we have seldom heard equalled." Because Lincoln was the only Illinois Whig in the House of Representatives, the paper referred to him as the "Lone Star of Illinois."[6]

The *Herald,* whose editor apparently had not read his rivals' advertisements of the rally, said that "without any previous notice," a large Whig meeting was held on Bromfield Street, during which "a strong, spontaneous demonstration" was made in favor of Taylor. Lincoln, said the paper, gave a speech "calculated to beat the disaffection among those who have left the Whig ranks and taken a stand on the Buffalo platform."

As for Lincoln's style and content, the *Herald* reporter thought that, "His remarks were well directed, and in his allusions to Van Buren he was exceedingly happy. He compared him to a man having a gun which went off at both ends — that he would kill the object in view and those who supported him, at the same time."[7]

His talk had lasted more than an hour and a half, so it was late by the time Lincoln returned to his room at the Tremont House. As he completed his fourth day in Massachusetts he could look back on four speeches which had been well received by those Whigs who had heard them. Tomorrow he would visit the child of the Cotton Whigs, Lowell.

CHAPTER VI
LOWELL

It is doubtful whether any city in Massachusetts underwent such profound change as did Lowell. What in 1820 had been quiet pastureland bordered by the Concord and Merrimack Rivers, was by 1848 a throbbing industrial city of 33,000 people. Francis Cabot Lowell, for whom the city was named, died before the first foundations were laid and never saw the place. He would have been stunned by its growth.[1]

The Boston Associates were indeed pleased by the progress of the mills and factories. Begun in the early 1820s, the city expanded quickly, so by 1848 its industries were capitalized at about $8,000,000. The factories used 35,000,000 pounds of cotton a year to turn out some 80,000,000 yards of cloth. Standing watch over the machines were 9,000 mill girls, and slightly less than half as many men.[2]

Yet even twenty years after its founding Lowell was beginning to taste a few of the social problems experienced by many mill towns. Immigration had helped to swell the population and shantytowns called "New Dublin" and "Paddy's Camp Lands" were sometimes troublesome.[3] Lucy Larcom, in her book *A New England Girlhood,* described the "shanty-like shops" which bordered Main Street. "The town had sprung up with a mushroom-rapidity," she wrote, "and there was no attempt at veiling the newness of its bricks and mortar, its boards and paint." She particularly remembered that "straggling petitioners for 'cold victuals' hung around our back yard, always of Hibernian extraction."[4]

Lowell was the political center of the area, and in spite of its dependence on conservative money, the Whigs here were not satisfied with Taylor's nomination any more than they were in other Bay State cities. Even before the Philadelphia convention the Lowell *Courier,* a Whig paper, asked: "Must not the Whig party, with General Taylor for a candidate, give up all pretense of holding a position against the aggressions of slavery?" After the nomination, the editor said that ". . . many firm Whigs here, and elsewhere, we are satisfied have . . . been disappointed."[5] As election day moved closer that disappointment ripened into a lethargy which truly worried Whig leaders, for it threatened to keep votes away from Taylor and thereby help the Democrats.

Lincoln's appearance in Lowell was advertised in the *Courier* on September 16. In calling Whigs to the City Hall, the editor said, "From what we learn our citizens depend upon enjoying a very high treat and hearing sound doctrine from able, staunch, and faithful Whigs."[6]

Just how many Lowellites were attracted to Lincoln's speech by the newspaper piece is not certain, but we do know of one who learned of it in another way. Samuel Hadley, sixteen years old, was walking up Central Street when he spied a poster hanging on a nearby wall. It was about a yard long and two feet wide, and it whetted his curiosity enough for him to stroll over for a closer look. It was a political poster, written in large block letters. It said:

WHIG MEETING
Next Saturday Evening — Sept. 16, at 7:30 o'clock
at City Hall

The Whigs of Lowell and Vicinity will be addressed next Saturday evening, by Hon. A. Lincoln of Illinois the only Whig Rep. in Congress, from that State, and George Woodman, Esq. of Boston.

All the Van Buren converts are respectfully invited to attend.

Galleries reserved for the ladies. Per Order the Whig Central Committee.

Linus Child, Chairman
Alfred Gilman, Sec'y.

Lowell City Hall, circa 1848. COURTESY OF THE LOWELL HISTORICAL SOCIETY.

Young Hadley, by his own admission "reared under Democratic influences," would ordinarily have paid no attention to such Whig propaganda, but the name Lincoln "sounded well," so he decided to investigate further.[7]

It was a pleasant evening as the boy walked into town. When he turned the corner at Carlton and Hovey's drugstore he heard shouts and laughter coming from the City Hall, in those days located upstairs in that business block. Upon reaching the second floor he noticed that the hall was well filled with a seated crowd. There was a good deal of laughter and Hadley saw that the gallery was occupied by a great number of ladies who also seemed to be having a good time. Looking at the platform, he recognized Linus Child, Homer Bartlett and a few other Lowell Whigs. He had arrived too late to hear George Woodman's brief speech but was just in time for Lincoln.

Young Samuel, who would one day become a distinguished Lowell judge, could not know it, but he was about to witness a scene which he would remember for the rest of his life. He was to be one of the relatively few New Englanders ever to see Abraham Lincoln deliver a stump speech. It is best described in Hadley's own words. Up on the platform he saw a

tall man about forty years of age, clothed in dark clothing, wearing a collar which turned over a black silk cravat, over six feet in height, slightly stooping as tall men sometimes are, with long arms, which he frequently extended in earnest gesticulation, of dark complexion with dark almost black hair, with strong and homely features, with sad eyes which now kindled into brightness in earnest argument, or quiet humor, and then assumed a calm sadness; a forceful and candid man I thought him rather than an eloquent one; he pointed his arguments with amusing illustrations, and funny stories, which he seemed to enjoy as he told them, for he joined in a comical way in the laugh they occasioned, shaking his sides, which peculiar manner seemed to add to the good humor of the audience; with a voice of more than average compass, clear and penetrating, pronouncing many of his words in a manner not usual to New England.

The speech lasted about forty-five minutes and at its end there was loud applause. Hadley saw George Woodman lean over and whisper something to Lincoln, who nodded and stepped forward again. He said, "Fellow citizens, I have been requested by my friend, Mr. Woodman, to say a few words to you in regard to the availability of General Taylor as a candidate of the Whig party for the Presidency." At that point Lincoln took ten more minutes to stress again why Taylor was a creditable candidate for the Whigs. Hadley said that as he left the hall he heard many complimentary remarks about the speech from the audience, and he hurried home to tell his family some of Lincoln's funny stories.[8]

There were four newspaper articles reviewing the Lowell address. On Monday, September 18, the *Courier* ran two accounts, both written by loyal Whigs. The first, by Alfred Gilman, said that it would be an injustice to the speech to give only a sketch of it, but said that it was "replete with good sense, sound reasoning and irresistible argument, and spoken with that perfect command of manner and matter which so eminently distinguishes the western orators." Gilman reported that Lincoln showed "in a masterly manner the inconsistency of those Whigs, who, being drawn off from the true and oldest Free Soil organization known . . . would lend their influence to help Mr. Van Buren . . . ."[9]

The second *Courier* story was written by Corporal L. R. Streeter, who had shared the platform with Lincoln. He noted that City Hall had been filled to capacity, with many seats taken by " . . . fair ladies — all true Whigs." Lincoln's had been a "most able speech," delivered in a "masterly and convincing manner." His message, said Streeter, was that "it is the first duty of Whigs to stand united and labor with devotion" to defeat the Democrats. The audience apparently agreed because, according to the *Courier,* Lincoln was frequently interrupted by "bursts of warm applause."[10]

The Boston *Atlas* carried an article on Tuesday, September 19, which said that the Lowell Whigs had "one of the tallest meetings on Saturday night that they have yet held." "The work," said the *Atlas*, "goes bravely on."[11]

The Lowell *Advertiser,* a Democratic paper, admitted that there was a "goodly number present," but " . . . in all those elements that make up an effective political demonstration . . . this meeting was vastly inferior to . . . those Whig assemblages which in years before have been convened in this city . . . ."[12]

The meeting had adjourned long after the last train had departed for Boston, so Lincoln spent the night and all day Sunday in Lowell. He may have been the guest of either Linus Child or Homer Bartlett, but more than likely he stayed with Stedman Hanks, a local minister reputed to be a relative of Lincoln's mother, Nancy Hanks.[13] If he was the minister's guest, it must have been an interesting visit for Lincoln. It seems that his kinsman was a good deal more liberal than the Illinoisian. Hanks was heavily involved in both the temperance and abolition movements. In 1852 he lost his pastorate, and several years later one of his successors said that Hanks had spent too much time talking about "rum and niggers" and not enough time preaching the Gospel.[14]

However pleasant the visit, Lincoln returned to Boston on Monday, September 18. He was in the city just long enough to make arrangements to go to Dorchester for an evening speech there.

CHAPTER VII
DORCHESTER AND CHELSEA

There are, unfortunately, two stops on Lincoln's tour of which little is known. These are his visits to Dorchester and Chelsea. They were poorly reported at the time and many interesting questions have been left unanswered.

His speech in Dorchester, given on September 18, was well advertised beforehand. On Saturday, two days before the rally, four Boston dailies, the *Atlas,* the *Courier,* the *Herald* and the *Advertiser* all ran the same notice: "The Hon. Abram Lincoln [sic], of Illinois, and the Hon. George Lunt, of Boston, will address the citizens of Dorchester on Monday evening next, Sept. 18th, at Richmond Hall."[1] A good indication of Lincoln's prior fame in Massachusetts is the fact that most Boston newspapers continued to misspell his name throughout his entire trip.

One newspaper which took note of the Dorchester speech before it was given was Samuel Bowles' *Springfield Republican.* On the day of the rally this journal reported that Lincoln, "who spoke so ably and interestingly at the Worcester Convention, addressed a great Whig meeting in New Bedford on Thursday evening, and is to speak to the Dorchester Whigs tonight." Lincoln, said the *Republican,* "is a very effective orator, and in hight [sic] is almost a match for 'Long John' Wentworth of his own State." Word of Lincoln's unusual speaking style was getting around because the writer said, "We hope he won't go home without giving us in this part of the State the benefit of his sound arguments and practical instruction."[2]

Dorchester lies south of Boston and in 1848 it was home to over 7,000 people.[3] Lincoln rode down there by carriage and arrived at about 8 p.m. His speech was given in Richmond Hall, on the corner of Washington Street and Churchill Place.

Nathaniel Safford, a local Whig, introduced Lincoln that evening. He said that the visitor was one of the Hingham

Lincolns, as well as a descendant of General Benjamin Lincoln. The Illinoisian disclaimed descent from the Revolutionary general and, according to William Herndon, playfully said that in his home state he had tried to introduce the principles of the Lincolns of Massachusetts. The audience, wrote Herndon, was struck by Lincoln's great height in the low-studded hall.[4]

The next day the Boston *Courier* reported a "full and enthusiastic" meeting, but said little more. This was the only available newspaper account of the Dorchester appearance.[5] Likewise, we know that Lincoln spent the night of September 18 at Stafford's beautiful house, on the corner of Washington and Morton Streets, a short distance from Richmond Hall, but nothing more is known of the visit.

The next day, Tuesday, September 19, Lincoln spoke in Chelsea, just north of Boston. That day's edition of the Boston *Atlas* contained a small notice giving the time and place of the meeting. Lincoln was to speak in Gerrish Hall, which the previous evening had been used for a Free Soil speech by Charles Sumner.[6]

The *Atlas* of September 20 had the only press coverage of the Chelsea appearance. "The Hon. Abraham Lincoln," said the writer, "made a speech which for aptness of illustration, solidity of argument and genuine eloquence is hard to beat."[7]

· Since there was no train service to Chelsea until 1854, Lincoln traveled to and from Gerrish Hall by carriage.[8] The next morning he made ready to meet a young Whig journalist who would take him to Dedham.

CHAPTER VIII
DEDHAM

In the early afternoon of September 20, George Monroe, a twenty-two year old newspaperman, went to the Tremont House to meet Abraham Lincoln and escort him to Dedham. They walked to the Pleasant Street depot of the Boston and Providence Railroad and arrived in time to catch the 3:30 train. The trip lasted about thirty minutes and before long Monroe began to worry about his guest. Lincoln, he wrote, seemed "awkward and ill at ease." During the entire trip he hardly said a word.[1] If the community to which he was traveling interested him at all, he hardly let it show.

The first half of the nineteenth century had seen Dedham become a prosperous little manufacturing center whose excellent location made it a travel center as well. Just southwest of Boston, its population in 1848 had swelled to 3,600 people. In that year the town boasted two cotton mills, three woolen mills, a shovel factory, a furnace for iron castings, a paper mill, a silk mill and several furniture factories, which alone employed over 500 workers.[2]

Before industry came to Dedham the people were strongly anti-Federalist and supported Jefferson, Madison and Monroe. The success of the factories, however, made them more conservative and John Quincy Adams, Henry Clay and William Henry Harrison became the new heroes.

Dedham was yet another Whig stronghold where the people wanted to remain loyal to the party but were unhappy with the nomination of an inexperienced candidate who was a slaveholder as well. After the Philadelphia convention had announced its decision, the *Norfolk Democrat* facetiously reported that in Dedham, "The Whigs here do not appear to relish the nomination of Taylor over much."[3]

When Lincoln's train pulled into the depot there was a brass band on hand to escort him to the Haven House, on the corner of High and Ames Streets. At that moment a reporter, calling himself "Hancock," was writing about the Whig festivities. He described the scene:

> While I write, a delegation from Roxbury is just marching to the Hall preceded by a full band of music and appropriate banners. The Hon. Mr. Lincoln, of Illinois, is expected to address the meeting. There is a good deal of enthusiasm, and a good spirit prevails here.[4]

The chances are good that Lincoln was a last minute addition to the program in Dedham. When the original notice of the Eighth District ratification meeting appeared in the Boston *Atlas,* his name was not listed among the speakers.[5] It seems probable that George Monroe had seen Lincoln at one of his other engagements and invited him to Dedham.

By the time the Whig cavalcade reached the Haven House, at that time owned by Freeman Fisher, the young newspaperman was regretting the invitation. The guest of honor seemed even more uncomfortable than before, and Monroe took this to mean that he found the atmosphere "this side of the mountains entirely uncongenial."

The Whig rally was held upstairs in Temperance Hall, on Court Street. Built in 1795, this had been Norfolk County's first court house. When the party arrived at the hall it was late in the afternoon and Monroe noticed that the place was only half-filled. Prospects were not bright, he thought, because Lincoln was an unknown and "there was nothing in his name particularly to attract." As he was introduced, though, he changed dramatically. Again, because it is one of the few surviving accounts of Lincoln on the stump in Massachusetts, Monroe's story deserves to be told in his own words. When Lincoln stepped forward, Monroe saw that

> . . . almost instantly there was a change. His indifferent manner vanished as soon as he opened his mouth. He went right to his work. He wore a black alpaca sack, and he turned up the sleeves of this, and

Freeman Fisher House. COURTESY OF THE DEDHAM HISTORICAL
SOCIETY AND MUSEUM, DEDHAM, MASSACHUSETTS.

Temperance Hall. COURTESY OF THE DEDHAM HISTORICAL
SOCIETY AND MUSEUM, DEDHAM, MASSACHUSETTS.

then the cuffs of his shirt. Next he loosened his necktie, and soon after he took his necktie off altogether. All the time he was gaining upon his audience. He soon had it as by a spell. I never saw men more delighted. His style was the most familiar and off-hand possible. His eyes lighted up and changed the whole expression of his countenance. He began to bubble out with humor. But the chief charm in the address lay in the homely way he made his points. There was no attempt at eloquence or finish of style. But for plain pungency of humor it would have been difficult to surpass his speech.[6]

The talk continued for about thirty minutes, when suddenly the clanging of a locomotive bell was heard. Lincoln told the crowd that he had to be on that train in order to make a later speaking engagement in Cambridge. Cries of "No! No! Don't stop!" came from all over the hall, and one man even promised to hitch up his horses and drive Lincoln over to Cambridge later, if only he would continue. Lincoln, however, remained steadfast, saying, "I have agreed to go to Cambridge and I must be there. I came here as I agreed, and I am going there in the same way." With that he was out the door and off to the depot.[7]

Lincoln had surprised no one in the audience more than the young reporter who had accompanied him. George Monroe went on to have a distinguished career as a journalist, yet when he died in 1903 at the age of seventy-seven, one of his most cherished memories was of that day more than fifty years before, when he had brought Abraham Lincoln to Dedham.[8]

Predictably, the Whig press hailed the speech. The Boston *Atlas* said that Lincoln had addressed the assembly for an hour "in a very agreeable and entertaining manner." Likewise, the Boston *Courier* called it an "excellent" meeting, noting that Lincoln had been joined on the platform by Henry Dearborn, another sterling Whig.[9]

But the *Norfolk Democrat* saw it another way. This

reporter witnessed the arrival of the train from Boston carrying Monroe and "the Hon. Western member of Congress." The writer said that the procession numbered about 100 and it marched through the street with a brass band. "When opposite the Phoenix House," said the reporter, "nineteen individuals mustered courage enough to tell the procession that they could hurrah three times." As for Lincoln, he was "received with a good deal of enthusiasm by about a fifth of the audience, who appeared to do all the applause."

In a sharp critique of Lincoln's speech, the writer said:

What he said was in praise of General Taylor and against Mr. Van Buren, saying very little against Cass except he was worth a million and a half dollars. He said Mr. Van Buren could not carry a majority of votes in any county in the United States, and yet he directed his battery to him exclusively.

The *Democrat* ended by saying that although it supposed that Lincoln gáve great satisfaction to the Taylorites present, the meeting had left its reporter "absolutely nauseous."[10]

The Roxbury *Gazette,* another Free Soil paper, noted that Lincoln had spoken to the "friends and supporters of the Slaveholders' Candidate for the Presidency . . . ." In all, the *Gazette* found it "a melancholy display . . . ."[11]

Yet even as the different reporters checked their notes on the meeting, Lincoln was already gone from Dedham, well on his way back to Boston to prepare for yet another speech that evening.

CHAPTER IX
CAMBRIDGE

After having run a successful race for the train departing Dedham, Lincoln returned to the Boston and Providence Railroad depot near the Boston Common, arriving in the early evening. He walked across the city to the station of the Fitchburg Railroad on Causeway Street to catch another train. This one took him in a westerly direction, across the Charles River to Cambridge.[1]

This city, like so many others in Massachusetts, was feeling the effects of massive change. By 1848 its population was nearing 15,000.[2] In 1845, the town had supported ninety-four manufacturing firms, employing more than 1,200 workers. Three years later, as Lincoln arrived, this number was growing and would continue to expand through the next decade.[3]

It was in this period, too, that Cambridge took on its academic luster. Harvard College bloomed, attracted the intellectual and financial elite of the Commonwealth, though one writer has pointed out that the real money lived over in Boston and sent its sons to Harvard.[4] It was at this school that the acumen of many members of both Whig factions had been sharpened. It was here that Messrs. Adams, Sumner and Palfrey were trained for the professions of education, law and politics.

Cambridge was another unhappy Whig community. The *Cambridge Chronicle,* a non-partisan journal, admitted that, "Our staid city of Cambridge, too, is up to its head and ears in politics,"[5] and much of the noise was being made by disaffected Whigs.

Lincoln was scheduled to speak to a ratification meeting held in City Hall, then located on Norfolk Street. In advertising the rally the Boston *Atlas* pointed out that: "Cambridge is in the field for the REST OF THE CAMPAIGN. She is all right. Van Buren is no go."[6] There is evidence that much of this was wishful thinking.

51

Unfortunately, there was no one like George Monroe or Samuel Hadley to give us personal recollections of Lincoln in Cambridge. However the reporter for the *Atlas* was feeling particularly descriptive that night, and he left an interesting, albeit partisan, account.

A sudden shower had descended just before the meeting began, said the reporter, but it did nothing to dampen the enthusiasm of the Whigs present. It was, according to the writer, "one of those old-fashioned Whig gatherings, which it does a true Whig good to witness." He went on to say that:

> . . . when the Old Cambridge Taylor Club entered the hall with a splendid band of music, and were received with cheer upon cheer, until the rafters shook and the roof rang, it seemed as if the building could not possibly contain the numbers who thronged to enter it.

Lincoln, said the writer, was "a capital specimen of a 'Sucker' Whig, six feet at least in his stockings, and every way worthy to represent the Spartan band of the only Whig district in poor benighted Illinois." His speech was described as "plain, direct, convincing . . . a model speech for the campaign."

Lincoln was followed to the rostrum by Lucius H. Chandler of Chelsea. He made a short speech and then the meeting broke up with "three tremendous cheers for Chandler and Illinois."[7]

Since there was no late train from Cambridge, Lincoln may have returned to Boston by carriage, or he may have walked back, a practice common in the 1840s.[8]

Tomorrow he would return to southeastern Massachusetts, to Taunton.

CHAPTER X
TAUNTON

In Taunton the Whigs knew that they faced a tough battle. The party had always done well here, but in this campaign the Free Soilers were capturing a large segment of popular support. The town's delegation to the Worcester convention, men of money and conservative tastes, knew that the color of a Western stump speaker could only enhance their cause, so they invited Lincoln to speak in Taunton, Thursday, September 21.

This town, like most of the others which Lincoln saw, had been caught up in large scale industrialization. Beginning in 1806 when Silas Shepard built a cotton mill, the eyes and ears of Tauntonians became accustomed to the sights and sounds of manufacturing. By 1848 the population had reached 10,000, and they worked in some 200 businesses, ranging from silver, to tacks to locomotives.[1]

Lincoln left the Tremont House that Thursday morning and walked near the Boston Common again toward the Boston and Providence Railroad depot, near present day Park Square. The 11 o'clock train took him in a southerly direction toward Taunton, the Bristol County seat. He had to change trains in Mansfield, just as he had done on his way to New Bedford earlier in the trip, and arrived in Taunton at about 12:30 p.m. The Taunton railroad station in those days had the look of a New England church.

During the afternoon Lincoln gave a speech in Taunton's north end, the Whittenton section. He spoke in Mechanics Hall, a building owned by the debating club at Reed & Barton, Silversmiths. The building stood at the southeast corner of Hopewell and Danforth Streets. The speech was not carried in the local press and no record of it survives.

That same afternoon the *American Whig*, published in Taunton, printed an *Extra Sheet* which said:

GATHER WHIGS! At the meeting, this evening at

Seven ½ o'clock at Union Hall, Hon. Abraham Lincoln, Member of Congress from Illinois will address Whigs, and all other citizens of Taunton who will call, this (Thursday) evening, on topics connected with the Presidential contest.

This distinguished gentleman has visited a number of our most populous towns, at the solicitations of our Whig friends, and he has met with a most cordial reception. Let us give him one in Taunton. He comes from the Democratic State of Illinois, he is a champion of Free Soil and Free Speech, and will afford us the pleasure of a specimen of Western eloquence in favor of Taylor and Fillmore . . . ."[2]

The editor of the newspaper felt compelled to print an *Extra Sheet* advertising Lincoln's visit because he was embarassed by a mistake he had made. It seems that in the regular edition of the *American Whig,* published on September 21, the day of the speech, the paper erroneously reported that Lincoln had spoken the previous evening and that he "was met with a cordial reception."[3] One can imagine the chagrin of local Whig leaders upon learning that Lincoln's address had been commented upon in the press before he had even delivered it.

The editor of the *Whig* was J. W. D. Hall, and lest any twentieth century readers be tempted to underestimate his ability because of this one mistake, a second thought should be given him. In fact, Hall was one of the area's most astute political observers, as well as a first-rate writer. In early September, for example, he had predicted that come November Taylor would win the election by carrying fifteen states, and he named the states. He also said that Van Buren would get no electoral votes. Taylor won, carried the exact states that Hall had predicted, and Van Buren polled no electoral votes.[4]

Just as in the other places which Lincoln visited, Tauntonians lost no love for Taylor. The fledgling *Daily Gazette*, whose editor, Amos Kilton, would soon join the Free Soilers, said that with all due respect to Taylor's service to the country,

Mechanics Hall. IMAGE COURTESY OF CHARLES E. CROWLEY PHOTOGRAPHIC
CENTER, OLD COLONY HISTORY MUSEUM, TAUNTON, MASSACHUSETTS.

" . . . we should have preferred someone who had a larger share of experience in civil affairs . . . ." The editor was certainly correct when he predicted that "in this section of the country the canvass will be less spirited than in the two preceding Presidential elections." Less than a week later the newspaper reported that defections from the Whig party seemed to be "quite extensive," and in July the *Gazette* covered the Bristol County Free Soil Convention in Taunton and reported between 600 and 800 people present.[5]

Lincoln's speech that evening was given in Union Hall, upstairs over Foster and Lawton's general store. The building was located on Winthrop Street, between the Mill River and the present day Winthrop Street Baptist Church. This hall hosted many of Taunton's political gatherings.

The Taunton press provides us with by far the best coverage of Lincoln on the stump. The *Daily Gazette,* in a brief piece, said, "Mr. Lincoln is a genuine Sucker, and is well versed in the political tactics of the Western country. His speech was full of humor, and was mainly devoted to . . . Mr. Van Buren and the Free Soil Party. He said very little about Cass, whom he considered the most prominent opponent of Gen. Taylor."[6]

Again and again the Whig message was simple: Van Buren could not win; he could only hurt Taylor enough to give the election to Cass. Lincoln was not trying to keep people from voting *for* the Democrat. He was trying to keep them from voting *against* Taylor.

One of the best descriptive stories showing Lincoln on the stump was presented by the *Old Colony Republican,* a Taunton paper with Whig preferences. It deserves to be quoted at length. The reporter said:

> It was an altogether new show for us — a western stump speaker. His form, his height, proved him native to that clime. His manners, and the way he advanced upon his hearers and cultivated their acquaintance until he became perfectly familiar with

Samuel L. Crocker. IMAGE COURTESY OF CHARLES E. CROWLEY PHOTOGRAPHIC
CENTER, OLD COLONY HISTORY MUSEUM, TAUNTON, MASSACHUSETTS

them, can any man think of without being tickled?

Leaning himself up against the wall, as he commenced, and talking in the plainest manner, and in the most indifferent tone, yet gradually fixing his footing, and getting command of his limbs, loosening his tongue, and firing up his thoughts, until he had got entire possession of himself and of his audience, were done in a style that will long be remembered.

Argument and anecdote, wit and wisdom, hymns and prophecies, platforms and syllogisms, came flying before the audience like wild game before the fierce hunter of the prairie. It was altogether an admirable speech and was listened to with the most vivid attention.

We never saw a more spirited meeting, the hall was well filled, and the greatest enthusiasm prevailed. There has been no gathering of any party in a region where the responses of the audience were so frequent and so vigorous.[7]

This picture is remarkably similar to one written by Lincoln's law partner, William Herndon, who had occasion to observe him in courtrooms and on campaign platforms all across Illinois.[8]

The most extensive, and the most scathing, newspaper account of Lincoln's entire Massachusetts tour was published in Taunton's *Bristol County Democrat* eight days after the speech. The writer was Dr. William Gordon, a cantankerous old Free Soiler who took Lincoln apart on virtually everything he said. The article, much longer and much more substantive than any other Bay State critique, said that the speech and the speaker gave "unlimited satisfaction to the disheartened Taylorites." "It was reviving," wrote Gordon, "to hear a man speak as if he believed what he was saying, and had a grain or two of feeling mixed up with it . . . ." Yet, he wrote, "When political spite runs high nothing can be too pungent or severe, and the speaker is appreciated in proportion as his statements

58

are rash and unscrupulous. So it was on this occasion."

Dr. Gordon took note of Lincoln's unusual style, even though he strongly disagreed with what he said. He wrote that:

> The speaker was far inferior as a reasoner to others who hold the same views, but then he was more unscrupulous, more facetious, and with his sneers he mixed up a good deal of humor. His awkward gesticulations, the ludicrous management of his voice, and the comical expression of his countenance, all conspired to make his hearers laugh at the mere anticipation of the joke before it appeared.

The reporter then went on to discuss the substance of Lincoln's arguments and, since the Whig case for Taylor had never been a strong one, he demolished them point by point. At one time he chastised Lincoln for telling a "whopper" about a statement made by Taylor, and several times he accused him of intellectual dishonesty. About the best thing he could say for Lincoln's address was that it had been given with an eye toward political expediency to help a sagging cause.[9]

Since there was no late train back to Boston, Lincoln spent the night in Taunton. Although it is not known for sure, it seems probable that he was the guest of either Samuel L. Crocker or Francis Baylies. Crocker was president of the local Taylor Club and a former Congressman. He lived in a stately mansion on Taunton Green and in 1960 his great granddaughter said that as a child she had been told that Lincoln was a guest in the house in 1848.[10] Baylies, also an ex-Congressman, lived in a lovely stone cottage not far from Union Hall. He was a noted scholar who set a fine table and enjoyed a reputation for outstanding hospitality. Perhaps the fact that both of these men died before Lincoln gained national prominence accounts for why so little is known about where he stayed in Taunton.

At 11:15 the next morning he was at the Taunton depot awaiting the train which would carry him back to Boston. A final rally that evening would climax his New England tour.

William H. Seward, circa 1848. LIBRARY OF CONGRESS.

CHAPTER XI
BOSTON: TREMONT TEMPLE

Abraham Lincoln's trip to Massachusetts was to end with a giant Whig rally in Boston. Once the staunchest of Whig strongholds, the city was now feeling the presence of the Free Soil movement. In addition to this, the general unpopularity of Taylor's candidacy was tarnishing the luster of past Whig victories. The old-timers did their best to make it seem that all was well, but it was evident that the usual campaign enthusiasm was lacking this year.

The party was taking a good deal of criticism from the rival press over Taylor's background, and there was no suitable answer which could be made. The Boston *Post,* a Democratic newspaper, saw Taylor as " . . . a man who the Whigs themselves admit possesses neither the experience nor the knowledge requisite to the intelligent discharge of that responsible office." The *Post* hit a tender spot when it said:

> Again, the Whigs of Massachusetts have been denouncing slavery and slaveholders — slaveocracy, as they call it — with all their wanted vehemence, and now for the suffrages of their party a man who owns, it is said, two hundred men, women and children![1]

With one simple statement the Boston *Evening Transcript,* itself a Whig journal which had supported Henry Clay, laid bare the deepest Whig strategy of 1848: "The prevailing sentiment among Whigs," said the editor, "appears to be this: 'Let us go into the contest, if at all, with the assurance of victory. No more defeats!' " "It is their superstition," said the *Transcript*, "that with Taylor, victory is secure."[2]

On Friday, September 22, as Lincoln returned to Boston from Taunton, his appearance that evening had already been well advertised. The Whig rally was to be keynoted not by Lincoln, but rather by the former Governor of New York, William H. Seward. On September 21 the Boston *Atlas,* in announcing the meeting, expressed fears that the affair might have to be held outdoors because all the public halls had been rented by the Van Burenites.[3]

The *Atlas'* fears were realized, for the next day's edition announced that the rally would be held outside in Court Square, located between City Hall and the Court House, at 7 o'clock that evening. In naming the speakers, Seward, "Abram Lincoln [sic]," Abbott Lawrence and Richard Fletcher, the *Atlas* said that, "We can add nothing to the force which these names have, to induce Whigs to turn out and listen."[4] Other notices of the rally were carried in the *Daily Advertiser,* the *Courier* and the *Springfield Republican.*[5]

There is no record of how Lincoln spent that Friday afternoon before his speech. The Whig press, especially the *Atlas,* edited by Lincoln's acquaintance Schouler, would have made interesting reading. On September 20 this paper ran a story entitled "The True Whig Spirit in the West," in which were listed the names of party leaders in Kentucky, Indiana, Ohio and Illinois. In his home state Lincoln was not mentioned, just the name of his friend Edward Baker.

There appeared in the same edition an article which, if he read it, surely caused Lincoln some discomfort. It said:

> THE WORKING OF THIRD PARTYISM — In the seventh Congressional District, Illinois, Harris, a Locofoco slavery expansionist, was elected to Congress by a majority of 106 over Logan, a Whig free territory man, which was done by the third party giving 166 votes to their own candidate, whom they knew they could not elect.[6]

This was Lincoln's seat in Congress, and the Whigs had chosen Stephen T. Logan to succeed him. The fact, among others, that he had to run on Lincoln's record was not mentioned in the *Atlas.*

The Boston which Lincoln saw on that fall afternoon held many fascinating sights. A short distance from his hotel, over on the Common, a Dr. Morrill was launching his hot air

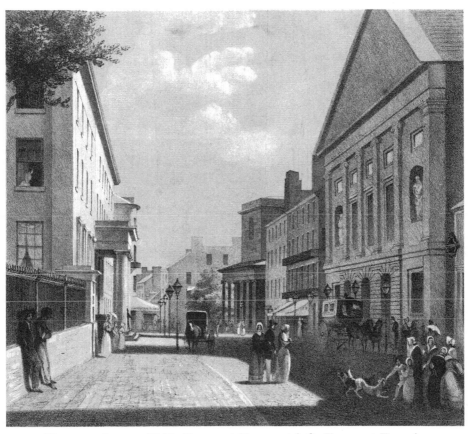

Tremont Street, 1843. Tremont House at left, Tremont Temple at right. COURTESY OF THE BOSTON PUBLIC LIBRARY, PRINT DEPARTMENT.

balloon, christened the *American Eagle,* on flights over the city. On that day he intended to take a young lady aloft with him to prove the extraordinary lifting power of the craft. The Boston Museum boasted "a half a million objects of interest," and over at Washington Hall, the site of Lincoln's first Boston speech, Sig Spinneito's 100 amazing canaries, each one performing "feats which appear incredible," could be seen for twelve and a half cents. Meanwhile the Horticultural Festival was also in town that day, and Seward was scheduled to make an afternoon appearance.[7]

By late afternoon it was pouring rain and it was evident that an open air meeting was out of the question. This was the only occasion during Lincoln's tour that the weather forced a change of plans. The problem was graciously solved by a Dr. Colton, who had rented the Tremont Temple, directly across the street from Lincoln's hotel. Colton was an inventor who traveled around lecturing on his products. He agreed to give up the hall that evening so that the Whigs could hold their meeting out of the rain.[8]

The Tremont Temple, built in 1829, was a plain building with a granite front and pillars placed over arched entrance doors. Constructed as a theater, it had been Boston's first opera house and had also seen the full gamut of theatrical programs. During its second season the theater had been managed by Junius Brutus Booth, the famous tragedian and father of John Wilkes Booth, but his stay was brief. More recently the building had been sold to the Baptist Society and it was often rented for lectures and concerts.[9]

With Dr. Colton out of the hall for the evening, the Whigs moved in, but the meeting still began thirty minutes late, at 7:30. The room was filled with people and the proceedings were called to order by William Hayden, who in his introduction fired the first blast at the Van Burenites. He said he was glad that the Whig party was now " . . . purged from those acrid humors and indigestible materials which had formerly lain hard on its stomach . . . ."[10]

64

When Hayden closed, George Lunt was chosen chairman and then introduced Seward. No greater contrast could have existed than that between Seward and the tall Illinoisian who sat with him on the platform. The former New York governor, elected to the Senate in 1848, was already a national figure, a recognized leader in the anti-slavery movement. His presence at a meeting guaranteed full attendance, and the Whig party was fortunate indeed to have his voice in this campaign.

Seward spoke very formally, and in his speech he tried to show how the Free Soil party was doing more harm than good in the fight against slavery. Third parties, he said, only served to draw off the Whigs' best talent. "Providence has permitted the people to be divided into only two great parties," he said, "not into half a dozen." If well intentioned people allowed themselves to be needlessly divided, then soon both major parties would be forced to "bow before the aristocracy of the South." As he concluded his lengthy address the audience burst into thunderous applause.[11]

Next, Lunt introduced Abraham Lincoln. It was late, almost 9:30 by the time he came forward, yet no one left the hall. He treated the Bostonians to the same speech that he had given in all of the other towns over the past ten days. The *Daily Advertiser's* man said that Lincoln "clearly and eloquently stated and maintained the Whig doctrine, that the Whigs are opposed to the extension of slavery, and believe that . . . General Taylor will do more to prevent such extension, than will . . . any other candidate . . . it is possible to elect . . . ." Lincoln also, said the paper, explained "the hopelessness and impossibility" of electing Van Buren. His remarks were "enthusiastically received."[12]

The Boston *Courier* said that Lincoln addressed the audience "in a most forcible and convincing speech, which drew down thunders of applause." In going after Van Buren, the paper said, "The hits which he gave the pseudo-Whigs, the skirts of the 'artful dodger' of Kinderhook were most capital." "It is a pity," said the reporter, "some of these gentlemen were not there to see how silly they look by the light of plain logic and common sense." The paper said that although the hour grew late, "his hearers listened with undiminished interest and satisfaction. He concluded amidst repeated rounds of deafening applause and the meeting adjourned at nearly half past ten o'clock."[13]

The Boston *Atlas* had less to say about Lincoln's part in the program. After fully reporting Seward's speech, Schouler merely said that Lincoln was greeted with great applause and made a "powerful and convincing speech, which was cheered to the echo." It was, thought Schouler, "one of the best meetings ever held in this good Whig city."[14]

Two other Boston papers, the *Herald* and the *Daily Mail,* briefly mentioned Seward but not Lincoln, and the *Post* did not report the meeting at all.[15]

September 22, 1848 was the last full day of Lincoln's campaign swing through Massachusetts. As he returned to the Tremont House that night he knew that after eleven days and twelve speeches he could put "Old Zack" in the background for a time and return to his wife and sons in Springfield, Illinois. Early on Saturday, September 23, he boarded a train of the Boston and Worcester Railroad which took him to Worcester. There he changed for a train which pointed him west, toward home.[16]

CHAPTER XII
EPILOGUE

The Whigs managed to hold their party together one last time in 1848, and Zachary Taylor went to the White House. He carried Massachusetts along the way, because in a conservative state where party loyalty ran deep, not enough Whigs could be shaken from the ranks to give any other candidate sufficient votes to matter. Of those towns where Lincoln spoke, for instance, Taylor lost only Worcester (and Worcester County) to Van Buren, and that by a margin of two to one. Yet an indication of Free Soil popularity is the fact that in those same places Van Buren beat Cass everywhere but in Boston and Cambridge.[1]

Whether Lincoln's help was important to Taylor's success is doubtful, for the Illinoisian was only one of a legion of stump speakers who crisscrossed the state, and it seems unlikely that an obscure prairie lawyer made much difference in the long run. Anyway, Taylor, like that other old Whig military hero, William Henry Harrison, died in office, and gone with him was the possibility that Lincoln would finish out his public life under the veil of political patronage.

Try as we may, we will find no trace in 1848 of any of the greatness which Lincoln would show in later years. Even Herndon admitted that in Massachusetts he "did not rise at any time above partisanship." He still needed a period of growth and maturing which would come to him in the 1850's.

Further, we can disagree with Herndon when he says that Lincoln left a "marked impression" on his Bay State audiences.[2] They certainly liked his style, and they seemed to like him as a person, but it is doubtful that many of them remembered him very long after the 1848 campaign. Indeed this writer, in a study of more than eighty-five newspapers from the six New England states, found that in 1860 not one editor made reference to Lincoln's speeches of a dozen years before.[3] For the most part it was only after he attained fame that his words of the Taylor campaign became important again.

In politics it is true that times change, and that enemies sometimes become friends, and friends enemies. When he stumped Massachusetts Lincoln supported the conservative Whigs. Yet many of them, including Robert C. Winthrop, George Lunt and others, failed to support him in 1860. Likewise he had hard words for the Free Soilers throughout that autumn. But many of the most ardent members of that party, men like Sumner, Wilson, Andrew and Dana became Republicans, and with their help he won the Presidency.[4]

It is ironic that most of those Bostonians jammed the Tremont Temple that night to hear William Seward, not Lincoln. Yet just twelve years later Lincoln would win the Republican presidential nomination at Seward's expense. The latter would go on to serve as an extremely able Secretary of State during the Civil War, and theirs was a friendship that deepened until Lincoln's death.

It is difficult to say who gained more from the experience, Abraham or the Yankees. For his part he saw and learned something about New England. When he returned home a newspaper said that he "was as much surprised that the people could subsist at all, on so cold and sterile soil, as he was at the grand, stupendous and comfortable appearance at every stop he moved."[5]

He also learned how much the slavery issue troubled New Englanders. Upon returning to the Tremont House after the last Boston rally, Lincoln said to Seward, "I reckon you are right. We have got to deal with this slavery question, and got to give more attention to it hereafter than we have been doing."[6]

Lincoln never gave another speech in Massachusetts. In 1860 he returned to New England, but for political reasons (the state's delegation to the upcoming Republican National Convention favored Seward) he skipped the Bay State and spoke only in Rhode Island, Connecticut and New Hampshire. Thus it was left to men like Samuel Hadley and George Monroe to remember what they had seen and heard of him here in 1848. Their memories, and a small piece from the Boston *Atlas*, prove what a truly masterful stump speaker he was. Three days after his Tremont Temple speech, William Schouler wrote the last word on Lincoln's Massachusetts tour. He said:

HON. ABRAHAM LINCOLN — In answer to the many applications which we daily receive from different parts of the State, for this gentleman to speak, we have to say that he left Boston on Saturday morning, on his way home to Illinois.[7]

Notes

Bibliography

Index

Notes

CHAPTER I
PRELUDE: THE WHIGS IN TURMOIL

[1] Harold U. Faulkner, "Political History of Massachusetts (1829-1851)," in *Commonwealth History of Massachusetts,* ed. Albert Bushnell Hart (New York: The States History Company, 1930), IV, 76; hereafter referred to as *Commonwealth History.*

[2] *Hand-Book for the Visiter [sic] to Lowell,* (Lowell: D. Bixby and Co., 1848), p. 30.

[3] John F. Sly, "Massachusetts in the National Government (1820-1861)," in *Commonwealth History,* IV, 281.

[4] Sly in *Commonwealth History,* IV, 281.

[5] Thomas H. O'Connor, *Lords of the Loom: The Cotton Whigs and the Coming of the Civil War* (New York: Charles Scribner's Sons, 1968), pp. 37-38.

[6] Kinley J. Brauer, *Cotton versus Conscience* (Lexington: University of Kentucky Press, 1967), p. 7.

[7] James Schouler, "The Whig Party in Massachusetts," *Massachusetts Historical Society Proceedings,* 50 (1916-1917), 40-41; Brauer, p. 19.

[8] Brauer, p. 19; O'Connor, pp. 66-67.

[9] Joseph G. Rayback, *Free Soil: The Election of 1848* (Lexington: University of Kentucky Press, 1970), p. 81.

[10] O'Connor, pp. 58-59.

[11] Donald Barr Chidsey, *The War with Mexico* (New York: Crown Publishers, Inc., 1968), p. 73.

[12] David Donald, *Charles Sumner and the Coming of the Civil War* (New York: Alfred A. Knopf, Inc., 1960), pp. 137-38.

[13] Donald, p. 140.

[14] Richard N. Current, *Daniel Webster and the Rise of National Conservatism* (Boston: Little, Brown & Co., 1955), p. 141.

CHAPTER II
OLD ROUGH AND READY

[1] James Morgan, *Our Presidents* (New York, 1958) quoted in Paul F. Boller, Jr., *Presidential Anecdotes* (New York: Oxford University Press, 1981), p. 103.

[2] Albert J. Beveridge, *Abraham Lincoln, 1809-1858* (Boston: Houghton Mifflin Co., 1928), I, 442.

[3] Brainerd Dyer, *Zachary Taylor* (New York: Barnes and Noble, Inc., 1967), p. 289.

[4] Donald W. Riddle, *Congressman Abraham Lincoln* (Urbana: University of Illinois Press, 1957), p. 103.

[5] Boston *Courier,* June 12, 1848, p. 2.

[6] Ernest McKay, *Henry Wilson, Practical Radical* (Port Washington, N.Y.: Kennikat Press, Inc., 1971), p. 66.

[7] Beveridge, I, 408.

[8] Roy P. Basler, ed., *The Collected Works of Abraham Lincoln* (8 vols. plus Index; New Brunswick: Rutgers University Press, 1953-1955), III, 29; hereafter cited as *Collected Works.*

[9] Abraham Lincoln to Archibald Williams, April 30, 1848, *Collected Works,* I, 467-68.

[10] Beveridge, I, 433.

[11] *Collected Works,* I, 467.

[12] Boston *Post,* June 9, 1848, quoted in Rayback, p. 205.

[13] Brauer, pp. 240-41.

[14] Boston *Daily Advertiser,* July 9, 1848, p. 2.

[15] Current, p. 155.

[16] Sidney Fisher, *The True Daniel Webster* (Philadelphia: J. B. Lipincott Co., 1911), p. 446.

[17] Boston *Daily Atlas,* June 9, 1848, p. 2.

[18] Rayback, p. 296.

CHAPTER III
WORCESTER

[1] The population figures are on file at the Worcester Historical Museum, while a good description of the election eve scene is found in the *Springfield Republican,* September 13, 1848, p. 2.

[2] Abraham Lincoln to William Schouler, August 8, 1848; August 28, 1848, *Collected Works,* I, 516.

[3] Abraham Lincoln to Junius Hall, September 3, 1848, quoted in Paul Findley, *A. Lincoln: The Crucible of Congress* (New York: Crown Publishers, Inc., 1979), p. 190.

[4] William H. Herndon and Jesse W. Weik, *Abraham Lincoln: The True Story of A Great Life* (New York: D. Appleton & Co., 1909), I, 276; hereafter referred to as Herndon.

[5] Mildred McClary Tymeson, *Worcester Centennial, 1848-1948* (Worcester: Worcester Centennial, Inc., 1948), p. 21.

[6] Tymeson, p. 20.

[7] *National Aegis* [Worcester, Mass.], June 14, 1848, p. 2.

[8] *Massachusetts Spy* [Worcester, Mass.], June 14, 1848, p. 2.

[9] Worcester *Palladium,* June 14, 1848, p. 2.

[10] Arthur P. Rugg, *"Abraham Lincoln in Worcester,"* Worcester Society of Antiquity, December 7, 1909, (Worcester: Belisle Printing and Publishing Co., 1914), p. 4.

[11] Worcester Bank and Trust Company, *Some Historic Houses of Worcester* (Boston: Walton Advertising and Printing Co., 1919), pp. 41-42.

[12] Rugg, p. 4.

[13] Findley, p. 190.

[14] Boston *Daily Advertiser,* September 14, 1848, p. 2.

[15] *Springfield Republican,* September 14, 1848, p. 2.

[16] Boston *Daily Advertiser,* September 14, 1848, p. 2.

[17] *Springfield Republican,* September 14, 1848, p. 2.

[18] *Springfield Republican,* September 14, 1848, p. 2.

[19] Boston *Daily Advertiser,* September 14, 1848, p. 2.

[20] *Springfield Republican,* September 14, 1848, p. 2.

[21] *Springfield Republican,* September 14, 1848, p. 2.

[22] *National Aegis* [Worcester, Mass.], September 20, 1848, p. 1.

[23] Boston *Atlas,* September 14, 1848, p. 2; Boston *Daily Advertiser,* September 14, 1848, p. 2; Boston *Courier,* September 14, 1848, p. 2.

[24] Worcester *Palladium,* September 20, 1848, p. 2.

[25] Henry J. Gardner to William Herndon, 1890, quoted in Rugg, p. 5.

[26] Rugg, p. 4.

[27] Rugg, pp. 9-10; Herndon, I, 283.

[28] *Springfield Republican,* September 14, 1848, p. 2; Boston *Atlas,* September 14, 1848, p. 2.

[29] *Massachusetts Spy* [Worcester, Mass.], September 20, 1848; September 22, 1848, quoted in Rugg, pp. 8-9.

[30] Rugg, p. 4.

[31] *Some Historic Houses of Worcester,* pp. 41-42; Rugg, pp. 7-8.

[32] E. L. Pierce to William Herndon, February 12, 1890, quoted in Rugg, p. 6.

[33] Charles Nutt, *History of Worcester and Its People* (New York: Lewis Historical Publishing Co., 1919), II, 579.

[34] Rugg, p. 5.

[35] Herndon, I, 289-91; Rugg, pp. 5-6.

CHAPTER IV
NEW BEDFORD

[1] The Boston theory is offered by Warren Jacobs in "Lincoln's Journeys on Massachusetts Railroads in 1848," an address delivered before the Lincoln Group of Boston, September 18, 1948. The Providence theory is presented in Jordan D. Fiore, *Abraham Lincoln Visits the Old Colony* (Taunton, Mass.: Old Colony Historical Society, 1978), pp. 4-6.

[2] Leonard Bolles Ellis, *History of New Bedford* (Syracuse: D. Mason & Co., 1892), p. 386; Hon. William W. Crapo, *Centennial in New Bedford* (New Bedford: E. Anthony & Sons, 1876), p. 101.

[3] *Atlas of New Bedford City, Massachusetts* (Boston: George H. Walker Co., 1881), p. 5; William M. Emery Papers, located in Genealogy Room of the New Bedford Free Public Library; Crapo, pp. 104-05.

[4] Ellis, p. 455.

[5] Emery Papers, New Bedford Free Public Library.

[6] New Bedford *Daily Mercury,* June 2, 1848, p. 2; June 12, 1848, p. 2.

[7] New Bedford *Daily Mercury,* September 14, 1848, p. 2.

[8] Ellis, p. 307.

⁹ New Bedford *Daily Mercury,* September 15, 1848, p. 2.

¹⁰ Zephaniah W. Pease, ed., *The Diary of Samuel Rodman: A New Bedford Chronicle of Thirty-Seven Years, 1821-1859* (New Bedford: Reynolds Printing Co., 1927), p. 287.

¹¹ Ellis, p. 74.

CHAPTER V
BOSTON: WASHINGTON HALL

¹ William S. Rossiter, "The Year Eighteen Forty Seven," in *Days and Ways of Old Boston,* ed. William S. Rossiter (Boston: R. H. Stearns and Co., 1915), pp. 14-17.

² Samuel Adams Drake, *Old Landmarks and Historic Personages of Boston* (Boston, 1872; rpt. Rutland, Vt.: Charles E. Tuttle, 1971), pp. 289-91.

³ Thomas Wentworth Higginson, "Other Days and Ways in Boston and Cambridge," in Rossiter, pp. 35-38.

⁴ Boston *Atlas,* September 15, 1848, p. 2; Boston *Courier,* September 15, 1848, p. 2.

⁵ Boston *Herald,* September 15, 1848, p. 4.

⁶ Boston *Atlas,* September 16, 1848, p. 2.

⁷ Boston *Herald,* September 16, 1848, p. 2.

CHAPTER VI
LOWELL

¹ Joseph W. Lipchitz, "The Golden Age," in *Cotton Was King: A History of Lowell, Massachusetts,* ed. Arthur L. Eno, Jr. (n.p.: New Hampshire Publishing Co., in collaboration with the Lowell Historical Society, 1976), pp. 80-82; *Hand-Book for the Visiter [sic] to Lowell,* p. 30.

[2] *Hand-Book,* pp. 8-9.

[3] Lipchitz, p. 99.

[4] Lucy Larcom, *A New England Girlhood* (Cambridge: Riverside Press, 1889), pp. 164-65.

[5] Lowell *Courier,* June 1, 1848, p. 2; June 12, 1848, p. 2.

[6] Lowell *Courier,* September 16, 1848, pp. 3-4.

[7] Samuel P. Hadley, "Recollections of Lincoln in Lowell in 1848 and Reading of Concluding Portion of the Emancipation Proclamation," in *The Abraham Lincoln Centennial* (Lowell: Lowell Historical Society, 1909), p. 370.

[8] Hadley, pp. 370-72.

[9] Lowell *Courier,* September 18, 1848, p. 2.

[10] Lowell *Courier,* September 18, 1848, p. 2.

[11] Boston *Atlas,* September 19, 1848, p. 2.

[12] Lowell *Advertiser,* September 19, 1848, p. 2.

[13] This information came to light in a 1927 letter to the editor of the Lowell *Courier,* in which Mrs. George P. Greenwood, of Billerica, Massachusetts claimed that her father's uncle, Linus Child, told her that Lincoln had boarded with the minister. Lowell *Courier,* October 24, 1927, now in the possession of the Lowell Historical Society.

[14] Frederick W. Coburn, *History of Lowell and Its People* (New York: Lewis Historical Publishing Co., 1920), I, 267.

CHAPTER VII
DORCHESTER AND CHELSEA

[1] Boston *Atlas,* September 16, 1848, p. 2; Boston *Courier,* September 16, 1848, p. 2; Boston *Advertiser,* September 16, 1848, p. 2; Boston *Herald,* September 16, 1848, p. 2.

[2] *Springfield Republican,* September 18, 1848, p. 3.

3 *History of the Town of Dorchester* (Boston: Ebenezer Clapp, Jr., 1859), p. 392.

4 Herndon, I, 285.

5 Boston *Courier,* September 20, 1848, p. 2.

6 Boston *Atlas,* September 19, 1848, p. 2; Herndon, I, 285.

7 Boston *Atlas,* September 20, 1848, p. 2.

8 Jacobs, p. 1.

CHAPTER VII
DEDHAM

1 George Monroe, "Lincoln's Visit to Dedham." Printed MS now in the collection of the Dedham Historical Society.

2 Herman Mann, *Annals of Dedham* (Dedham: Herman Mann, 1847), p. 61; Dedham Tercentenary Committee, *Dedham Tercentenary, 1636-1936* (Dedham: Transcript Press, 1936), p. 34.

3 *Norfolk Democrat,* June 16, 1848, p. 2.

4 Boston *Atlas,* September 21, 1848, p. 2.

5 Boston *Atlas,* September 18, 1848, p. 2.

6 Monroe MS.

7 Monroe MS.

8 Edward Stanwood, "Memoir of George Harris Monroe," *Massachusetts Historical Society Proceedings,* 50 (1916-1917), 34.

9 Boston *Atlas,* September 25, 1848, p. 2; Boston *Courier,* September 22, 1848, p. 2.

10 *Norfolk Democrat,* September 22, 1848, p. 2.

[11]   Roxbury *Gazette,* September 23, 1848, quoted in Walter Austin, *Tale of A Dedham Tavern: History of the Norfolk Hotel* (Cambridge: Riverside Press, 1912), p. 147.

CHAPTER IX
CAMBRIDGE

[1]   Jacobs, p. 1.

[2]   Lucius R. Paige, *History of Cambridge, Massachusetts, 1630-1877* (Cambridge: Riverside Press, 1877), p. 452.

[3]   S. B. Sutton, *Cambridge Reconsidered* (Cambridge: M.I.T. Press, 1976), p. 55.

[4]   Sutton, p. 50.

[5]   *The Cambridge Chronicle,* September 7, 1848, p. 3.

[6]   Boston *Atlas,* September 20, 1848, p. 2.

[7]   Boston *Atlas,* September 22, 1848, p. 2.

[8]   Higginson, p. 27.

CHAPTER X
TAUNTON

[1]   Edmund Hatch Bennett, "Historical Address," in *250th Anniversary of the Founding of Taunton, 1639-1889* (Taunton: Charles H. Buffington Press, 1889), pp. 70-71; Fiore, p. 9.

[2]   Fiore, p. 11.

[3]   *American Whig* [Taunton, Mass.], September 21, 1848, p. 2.

[4]   Fiore, p. 12.

[5]   Taunton *Daily Gazette,* June 10, 1848, p. 2; June 14, 1848, p. 2; July 31, 1848, p. 2.

[6] Taunton *Daily Gazette,* September 23, 1848, p. 2.

[7] *Old Colony Republican* [Taunton, Mass.], September 23, 1848, quoted in Sheldon H. Harris, "Abraham Lincoln Stumps A Yankee Audience," *New England Quarterly,* 38 (June, 1965), 230.

[8] Herndon, II, 74-75.

[9] *Bristol County Democrat* [Taunton, Mass.], September 29, 1848, pp. 2-3.

[10] Caroline A. Couch to Wallace Austin, May 25, 1960. MS now in the files of the Old Colony Historical Society, Taunton, Mass.

CHAPTER XI
BOSTON: TREMONT TEMPLE

[1] Boston *Post,* June 10, 1848, p. 2.

[2] Boston *Evening Transcript,* June 6, 1848, p. 2.

[3] Boston *Atlas,* September 21, 1848, p. 2.

[4] Boston *Atlas,* September 22, 1848, p. 2.

[5] Boston *Daily Advertiser,* September 22, 1848, p. 2; Boston *Courier,* September 22, 1848, p. 2; *Springfield Republican,* September 22, 1848, p. 2.

[6] Boston *Atlas,* September 20, 1848, p. 2.

[7] Boston *Daily Bee,* September 22, 1848, p. 2. This paper named all of the places of entertainment in Boston.

[8] Boston *Herald,* September 23, 1848, p. 4.

[9] Drake, pp. 291-93.

[10] Boston *Courier,* September 23, 1848, p. 2.

[11] Boston *Atlas,* September 23, 1848, p. 2.

[12] Boston *Daily Advertiser,* September 23, 1848, p. 2.

13 Boston *Courier,* September 23, 1848, p. 2.

14 Boston *Atlas,* September 23, 1848, p. 2.

15 Boston *Herald,* September 23, 1848, p. 2; Boston *Daily Mail,* September 23, 1848, p. 2; Boston *Post,* September 23, 1848, p. 2.

16 Jacobs, p. 2.

CHAPTER XII
EPILOGUE

1 Boston *Atlas,* November 8, 1848, p. 2.

2 Herndon, I, 286.

3 William F. Hanna, "Abraham Lincoln and the New England Press, 1858-1860," Diss. Boston College, 1980.

4 Herndon, I, 287.

5 *American Whig* [Taunton, Mass.], November 16, 1848, p. 2.

6 Ida M. Tarbell, "Lincoln in Congress," *McClure's Magazine,* May, 1896, p. 544.

7 Boston *Atlas,* September 25, 1848, p. 2.

Bibliography

MANUSCRIPTS

Emery, William M. Emery Papers. Genealogy Room,
New Bedford Free Public Library, New Bedford, Mass.

Monroe, George. "Lincoln's Visit to Dedham." MS.
Dedham Historical Society, Dedham, Mass.

LETTERS

Couch, Caroline A. Letter to Wallace Austin. 25 May 1960.
Old Colony Historical Society, Taunton, Mass.

Greenwood, Mrs. George P. Letter to Editor,
Lowell *Courier.* 24 October 1927.
Lowell Historical Society, Lowell, Mass.

PRINTED PRIMARY SOURCES

Basler, Roy P., ed. *The Collected Works of Abraham
Lincoln.* 8 vols. New Brunswick: Rutgers University Press,
1953-55.

Hand-Book for the Visiter to Lowell. Lowell: D. Bixby and
Co., 1848.

Herndon, William H., and Jesse W. Weik. *Abraham Lincoln:
The True Story of A Great Life.* 2 vols. New York: D.
Appleton & Co., 1909.

Larcom, Lucy. *A New England Girlhood.* Cambridge:
Riverside Press, 1889.

Pease, Zephaniah W., ed. *The Diary of Samuel Rodman: A
New Bedford Chronicle of Thirty-Seven Years, 1821-1859.*
New Bedford: Reynolds Printing Co., 1927.

SECONDARY SOURCES

Atlas of New Bedford City, Massachusetts. Boston: George H. Walker, Inc., 1881.

Austin, Walter. *Tale of A Dedham Tavern: History of the Norfolk Hotel.* Cambridge: Riverside Press, 1912.

Beveridge, Albert J. *Abraham Lincoln, 1809-1858.* 2 vols. Boston: Houghton-Mifflin Co., 1928.

Boller, Paul F. *Presidential Anecdotes.* New York: Oxford University Press, 1981.

Bauer, Kinley J. *Cotton versus Conscience.* Lexington: University of Kentucky Press, 1967.

Chidsey, Donald Barr. *The War With Mexico.* New York: Crown Publishers, Inc., 1968.

Coburn, Frederick W. *History of Lowell and Its People.* New York: Lewis Historical Publishing Co., 1920. Vol. I.

Crapo, William W. *Centennial in New Bedford.* New Bedford: E. Anthony & Sons, 1876.

Current, Richard N. *Daniel Webster and the Rise of National Conservatism.* Boston: Little, Brown & Co., 1955.

Dedham Tercentenary Commission. *Dedham Tercentenary, 1636-1936.* Dedham: Transcript Press, 1936.

Donald, David. *Charles Sumner and the Coming of the Civil War.* New York: Alfred A. Knopf, Inc., 1960.

Drake, Samuel Adams. *Old Landmarks and Historic Personages of Boston.* 1872; rpt. Rutland, Vt.: Charles E. Tuttle, Co., 1971.

Dyer, Brainerd. *Zachary Taylor.* New York: Barnes and Noble, Inc., 1967.

Ellis, Leonard Bolles, *History of New Bedford.* Syracuse: D. Mason & Co., 1892.

Faulkner, Harold U. "Political History of Massachusetts (1829-1851)." In *Commonwealth History of Massachusetts.* Ed. Albert Bushnell Hart. New York: The States History Co., 1930. Vol. IV, pp. 74-102.

Findley, Paul. *A. Lincoln: The Crucible of Congress.* New York: Crown Publishers, Inc., 1979.

Fiore, Jordan D. *Abraham Lincoln Visits the Old Colony.* Taunton, Mass.: Old Colony Historical Society, 1978.

Fisher, Sidney. *The True Daniel Webster.* Philadelphia: J. B. Lippincott Co., 1911.

Higginson, Thomas Wentworth. "Other Days in Boston and Cambridge." In *Days and Ways of Old Boston.* Ed. William S. Rossiter. Boston: R. H. Stearns & Co., 1915, pp. 27-38.

History of the Town of Dorchester. Boston: Ebenezer Clapp, Jr., 1859.

Lipchitz, Joseph W. "The Golden Age." In *Cotton was King: A History of Lowell, Massachusetts.* Ed. Arthur L. Eno, Jr. n.p.: New Hampshire Publishing Co., 1976, pp. 80-103.

McKay, Ernest. *Henry Wilson, Practical Radical.* Port Washington, N.Y.: Kennikat Press, 1971.

Mann, Herman. *Annals of Dedham.* Dedham: Herman Mann, 1847.

Memoir of Joseph Grinnell. Daniel Clapp, Printer, 1863.

Nutt, Charles. *History of Worcester and Its People.* New York: Lewis Historical Publishing Co., 1919. Vol. II.

O'Connor, Thomas H. *Lords of the Loom.* New York: Charles Scribners Sons, 1968.

Paige, Lucius R. *History of Cambridge, Massachusetts.* Cambridge: Riverside Press, 1877.

Rayback, Joseph G. *Free Soil: The Election of 1848.* Lexington: University of Kentucky Press, 1970.

Riddle, Donald W. *Congressman Abraham Lincoln.* Urbana: University of Illinois Press, 1957.

Rossiter, William S. "The Year Eighteen Forty Seven." In *Days and Ways in Old Boston.* Ed. William S. Rossiter. Boston: R. H. Stearns & Co., 1915, pp. 11-25.

Sly, John F. "Massachusetts in the National Government (1820-1861)." In *Commonwealth of Massachusetts.* Ed. Albert Bushnell Hart. New York: The States History Company, 1930. Vol. IV, pp. 281-308.

Sutton, S. B. *Cambridge Reconsidered.* Cambridge: M.I.T. Press, 1976.

Tymeson, Mildred McClary. *Worcester Centennial, 1848-1948.* Worcester: Worcester Centennial, Inc., 1948.

Worcester Bank and Trust Company. *Some Historic Houses of Worcester.* Boston: Walton Advertising and Printing Co., 1919.

JOURNALS

Harris, Sheldon H. "Abraham Lincoln Stumps a Yankee Audience." *New England Quarterly,* 38 (1965), pp. 227-33.

Schouler, James. "The Whig Party in Massachusetts." *Massachusetts Historical Society Proceedings,* 50 (1916-1917), pp. 39-53.

Stanwood, Edward. "Memoir of George Harris Monroe." *Massachusetts Historical Society Proceedings,* 50 (1916-1917), pp. 30-36.

Tarbell, Ida M. *The Life of Abraham Lincoln,* "Lincoln in Congress." *McClure's Magazine,* May, 1896, pp. 526-44.

ADDRESSES

Bennett, Edmund Hatch. "Historical Address."
In *250th Anniversary of the Founding of Taunton.*
Taunton: Charles H. Buffington Press, 1889, pp. 29-77.

Hadley, Samuel P. "Recollections of Lincoln in Lowell in 1848
and Reading of Concluding Portion of the Emancipation
Proclamation." In *The Abraham Lincoln Centennial.*
Lowell: Lowell Historical Society, 1909, pp. 365-87.

Jacobs, Warren. "Lincoln's Journeys on Massachusetts Railroads in 1848." Address delivered before the Lincoln
Group of Boston, September 18, 1948.

Rugg, Arthur P. "Abraham Lincoln in Worcester." Address
delivered before the Worcester Society of Antiquity,
December 7, 1909. Worcester: Belisle Printing and Publishing Co., 1914.

Wahlstrom, Carl E. "Abraham Lincoln in Lowell." Address
delivered before the Lincoln Group of Boston, September
18, 1948.

DISSERTATIONS

Hanna, William F. "Abraham Lincoln and the New England
Press, 1858-1860." Diss. Boston College, 1980.

NEWSPAPERS

Boston *Atlas*
Boston *Courier*
Boston *Daily Advertiser*
Boston *Daily Bee*
Boston *Daily Mail*
Boston *Evening Transcript*
Boston *Herald*
Boston *Post*
Cambridge Chronicle
Norfolk Democrat [Dedham]

Lowell *Advertiser*
Lowell *Courier*
New Bedford *Daily Mercury*
Springfield Republican
American Whig [Taunton]
Bristol County Democrat [Taunton]
Taunton *Daily Gazette*
Massachusetts Spy [Worcester]
National Aegis [Worcester]
Worcester *Palladium*

Index

Created by Helene S. Ferranti

Page numbers in italics indicate illustrations.

Bryant, William Cullen, 4
Buffalo, NY, anti-slavery convention 1848, 10, 36
Bullock, Alexander (Worcester Whig), 14, 16, 21, 23
Burlingame, Anson, 3

Cambridge Chronicle, 51
Cambridge, MA, 1, 51–52
Cass, Lewis (1848 Democratic presidential nominee), 10, *15*, 18, 20, 50, 56
Chandler, Lucius (Chelsea), 52
Chelsea, MA, 1, 44
Chicopee, MA, 2
Child, Linus (Lowell Whig), 38, 40, 42
Choate, Rufus (Whig party leader), 3, 5, 23
Clay, Henry, 8, 18
Clay, Henry, Jr., 26
"Conscience Whigs": and abolitionism, 5–6, 10, 36; and Mexican War, 6; opposition to Taylor, 7–8, 10
cotton textile industry, Massachusetts: control of Whig party, 3; dependence on slavery, 3; growth of, 1–2, 28, 37, 53; and Texas annexation, 5–6
"Cotton Whigs": and Mexican War, 5–6; response to Taylor's nomination, 10, 12
Crocker, Samuel L. (Taunton Taylor Club), *57,* 59

Dana, Richard Henry, 3, 68
Dearborn, Henry (Dedham Whig), 49

Dedham, MA: dissatisfaction with Taylor's candidacy, 45; growth of, 45; Lincoln's demeanor, 45, 46, 49; Lincoln's speech in, 46, 49–50; as Whig stronghold, 45
Dorchester, MA, 43–44
Douglas, Stephen A., 8
Douglass, Frederick, 28

Earle, John Milton (*Massachusetts Spy* reporter), 21, 23
Everett, Edward (Whig party leader), 3

Fall River, MA, 2
Fillmore, Millard, 7
Free Soil party: and 1848 election results, 57; attacked by William Hayden, 64; in Boston, 61; and Charles Sumner, 44; and "Conscience Whigs," 10; formation of, 10; Lincoln's arguments against, 18–19, 34, 50, 56, 65; in New Bedford, 26; New England strength, 10, 21, 56, 61, 67; Seward's criticism of, 65; in Taunton, 53, 56; in Worcester, 13–14. *See also* Van Buren, Martin

Gardner, Henry J. (future Massachusetts governor): on Lincoln's exceptional memory, 26; on Lincoln's Worcester City Hall speech, 20
Garrison, William Lloyd, 28
Gerrish Hall, Chelsea, 44
Gilman, Alfred (Lowell Whig), 38, 41

Gordon, Dr. William, *Bristol County Democrat* opinion piece, 58–59

Grinnell, Joseph (New Bedford Congressman), *29*; Joseph Grinnell Mansion, *31*; as Lincoln's host, 30; reelection fight, 27; and Wamsutta Mills, 28

Hadley, Samuel, on Lincoln, 38, 40–41, 68–69

Hall, Junius (Boston attorney), 13, 16

Hall, J. W. D. (*American Whig* editor), 54

Hanks, Stedman (Lowell minister), 42

Harvard College, 51

Haven House (Freeman Fisher House), Dedham, 45, 46, *47*

Haverhill, MA, 2

Hayden, William (Boston Whig), 64

Herndon, William (Lincoln's law partner), 44, 58, 67

Holmes, Oliver Wendell, 33

Kellogg, Ensign H. (Pittsfield Whig), 16

Kilton, Amos (Taunton *Daily Gazette* editor), 54, 56

Larcom, Lucy, *A New England Girlhood*, 37

Lawrence, Abbott (Whig party leader), 3, 7

Lawrence, MA, 2

Lawrence, William (Whig party leader), 3

Lincoln, Abraham; arguments against Free Soil party, 18–19, 34, 50, 56, 65; description of, 16, 40, 45, 46, 49; exceptional memory, 26; on Henry Clay, 8, 18; historical context of Massachusetts trip, 1–6; influence on Massachusetts voters, 67–68; on Lewis Cass, 18, 20, 50, 56; on slavery issue, 19, 21, 34, 65, 68; speaking style, 40–41, 43, 46, 49, 56, 58, 59, 69; and "Young Indians," 8

Lincoln, Abraham (speeches): in Boston, 34, 36, 65–66; in Cambridge, 52; in Chelsea, 44; in Dedham, 46, 49–50; in Dorchester, 43–44; in Lowell, 38, 40–42; in New Bedford, 28, 30; in Taunton, 53–54, 56, 58–59; in Worcester, 16, 18–21, 23

Lincoln, George (son of Levi Lincoln), 26

Lincoln, Levi (former Massachusetts governor), *22*; Levi Lincoln House, 16, *24*, *25*; at Worcester Convention, 23, 26

Logan, Stephen T. (Illinois Whig), 62

Longfellow, Henry Wadsworth, 4

Lovejoy, Elijah (abolitionist editor), 21

Lowell *Advertiser*, 42

Lowell *Courier*: on Lincoln's speech, 41; promotion of Lincoln's speech, 38; on Taylor's candidacy, 37

Lowell, Francis Cabot, 1–2, 37

Lowell, James Russell, 4

Lowell, MA: City Hall, *39*; cotton textile industry, 2, 37; growth of, 1, 37; Lincoln's speech in, 38, 40–42; social problems, 37; Whig dissatisfaction with Taylor candidacy, 37–38

Lunt, George (Boston Whig), 43, 65, 68

Massachusetts: industrialization, 1–2; population growth, 1

Massachusetts cotton textile industry. *See* cotton textile industry, Massachusetts

Massachusetts Spy: position on Taylor, 14; on Worcester depot speeches, 21, 23

Massachusetts Whig party. *See* Whig party, Massachusetts

Mexican War: and Massachusetts Whig party divisions, 5–6; personal toll on Massachusetts Whig leaders, 27; and slavery issue, 6

Monroe, George (journalist), 45–46, 49, 68–69

New Bedford *Daily Mercury*: on Lincoln's Liberty Hall speech, 30; on Taylor's candidacy, 28

New Bedford, MA: abolitionism in, 28; cotton textile industry, 28; as Free Soil stronghold, 26; Lincoln's speech in, 28, 30; population, 27; Quaker influence in, 28, 30; railroad station, 27; whaling industry, 27

A New England Girlhood (Lucy Larcom), 37

Norfolk Democrat: on Lincoln's Dedham speech, 50; on Whig dissatisfaction, 45

Palfrey, John Gorham (former publisher *North American Review*), 3, 51

Parker, Theodore (abolitionist), 28

Phillips, Wendell (abolitionist), 28

Polk, James, 5

Quakers and slavery issue, 28

railroads: Boston and Providence Railroad, 45, 51, 53; Boston and Worcester Railroad, 66; Fitchburg Railroad, 51

Reed & Barton, 53

Reed, John (1848 Massachusetts Whig lieutenant governor nominee), 23

Richmond Hall, Dorchester, 43–44

Rodman, Samuel (Quaker diarist), 30

Roxbury *Gazette*, 50

Safford, Nathaniel (Dorchester Whig), 43–44

Schouler, William (Boston *Atlas* editor), 12, 13, 20, 69

Seward, William H., *60*, 61, 64, 65, 68

slavery issue: and Buffalo antislavery convention, 10, 36; and cotton textile industry, 3; and Free Soil party, 10; Lincoln on, 19, 21, 34, 65, 68; and Mexican War, 6; and Quakers, 28; and

Whig party divisions, 4–6, 37–38, 61; and "Young Indians," 8

Smith, Truman (Connecticut congressman), 8

Springfield Republican: on Lincoln as speaker, 43; on Lincoln's Worcester City Hall speech, 18, 19

Stephens, Alexander (future Confederacy Vice-President), 8

Streeter, Corporal L. R. (Lowell *Courier* reporter), 41

Sumner, Charles, 3–4, 44, 51, 68

tariff, protective: and James K. Polk, 5; Whig party's support of, 2

Taunton *American Whig*, advertisement of Lincoln, 54

Taunton *Bristol County Democrat*, critique of Lincoln's speech, 58–59

Taunton *Daily Gazette*: on Lincoln's speech, 56; on Taylor's candidacy, 54, 56

Taunton, MA: cotton textile industry in, 2, 53; Free Soil Convention, 56; growth of, 53; Mechanics Hall, *55*; railroad station, 53; Whig party divisions in, 53, 54, 56

Taunton *Old Colony Republican*, on Lincoln's speaking style, 56, 58

Taylor, Zachary, *9*; "Conscience Whigs" opposition to, 7–8, 10; election victory, 67; and J. W. D. Hall's prediction, 54; Lincoln's

defense of, 6, 8, 10, 18, 34, 41; nomination for presidency, 6–8; questionable qualifications, 7, 56, 61; as slave owner, 6–7, 61

Temperance Hall, Dedham, 46, *48*

Texas annexation: and Massachusetts cotton textile industry, 5–6; and Massachusetts Whig party divisions, 4–6

third parties: Boston *Atlas* on, 62; effect on elections, 62; Seward's criticism of, 65

Tremont House, *63*; Bill of Fare, 1847, *32*; as Lincoln's hotel, 33, 36, 45, 53, 64, 66; notable guests of, 33

Tremont Temple, *63*, 64

Tyler, John, 5

Van Buren, Martin, *11*; as Free Soil party nominee, 10; and J. W. D. Hall's prediction, 54; Lincoln on, 36. *See also* Free Soil party

Waltham, MA, 2

Webster, Daniel: justification for Taylor's nomination, 8, 12; on Mexican War, 5–6; and Texas annexation, 5; as Whig party leader, 3

Webster, Edward (son of Daniel Webster), 26

Whig party: 1848 campaign banner, *35*; composition of, 2; and Harvard College, 51; lack of platform, Lincoln's defense of, 18; strategy of, 61; support of protective tariff, 2

Whig party, Massachusetts: and
  1848 election results, 67; ascendancy of, 2–3; cotton textile
  industry control of, 3; dissidents,
  3–4; divisions within, 3–6,
  37–38, 51, 53, 54, 56, 61; leaders
  of, 3; and Mexican War, 5–6;
  response to Taylor nomination,
  7–8, 10, 12; state convention
  events, 21, 23, 26; support in
  Cambridge, 51–52; and Texas
  annexation, 4–5
Whittier, John Greenleaf, 4
Wilson, Henry, 3–4, 7, 68
Winthrop, Robert C. (Whig party
  leader), 3, 5, 23, 68

Woodman, George (Boston
  Whig), 40, 41
Worcester, MA: as 1848 Whig
  state convention site, 13–14;
  City Hall, *17*; as Free Soil party
  stronghold, 13–14, 21; growth
  of, 1, 14; Lincoln's speeches in,
  16, 18–21, 23
Worcester *National Aegis*: on
  Lincoln's Worcester City Hall
  speech, 19; position on Taylor, 14
Worcester *Palladium*: on Lincoln's
  Worcester City Hall speech, 20;
  position on Taylor, 14

"Young Indians," 8

William F. Hanna holds a PhD from Boston College and has taught United States history throughout his career. He is presently a visiting lecturer at Bridgewater State University and serves as president of the Old Colony History Museum in Taunton, Massachusetts. A past president of the Lincoln Group of Boston, he is also the author of *A History of Taunton, Massachusetts* and *Avon, Massachusetts, 1720–1988*. He speaks and writes widely on New England history.